The Witches Almanac

Spring 2024—Spring 2025

CONTAINING pictorial and explicit delineations of the
magical phases of the Moon together with information about astrological
portents of the year to come and various aspects of occult knowledge
enabling all who read to improve their lives in the old manner.

The Witches' Almanac, Ltd.

Publishers   Providence, Rhode Island
www.TheWitchesAlmanac.com

Address all inquiries and information to
THE WITCHES' ALMANAC, LTD.
P.O. Box 25239
Providence, RI   02905-7700

© 2023 BY THE WITCHES' ALMANAC, LTD.
All rights reserved

13-ISBN: 978-1-881098-95-9 The Witches' Almanac—Classic
13-ISBN: 978-1-881098-94-2 The Witches' Almanac—Standard
Español 13-ISBN: 978-1-881098-36-2 The Witches' Almanac—Standard
E-Book 13-ISBN: 978-1-881098-96-6 The Witches' Almanac—Standard

ISSN: 1522-3184

First Printing July 2023

Printed in USA

Established 1971 by Elizabeth Pepper

Preface

Astrology, an ancient practice rooted in celestial observations, has captivated humanity for centuries, and its value Astrology extends beyond just divination. Astrology has had a profound impact on individuals and cultures worldwide as a tool for self-reflection, personal growth and connection to humanity and the cosmos. From ancient civilizations to modern societies, Astrology has influenced art, science, politics, literature, war and both personal and cultural belief systems. Astrology has been used for centuries in the practice of magic, foretelling the weather, appeasing the Gods and even in choosing kings.

At its core, Astrology provides a symbolic language through which individuals can discover their personalities, strengths and weaknesses. The intricate interplay of planetary positions at the time of your birth offers insight into character traits, preferences and potential life paths. A student of Astrology could make an entire life study of just the Planets. Astrology empowers individuals to embrace their authentic selves and make informed choices aligned with their true natures as symbolically shown in the natal chart. In addition, Astrology is a language used by magicians to converse about subjects that require more than the ordinary linguistic.

Astrology fosters a profound connection between individuals and the vast cosmic universe. Humans are inherently connected to the celestial realm and Astrology provides a bridge to that connection. It reminds you that you are part of a grand cosmic tapestry in which celestial bodies and their positions and relationships with each other influence your life in subtle—and not so subtle—ways. This connection cultivates a sense of awe, wonder and reverence for the natural world, providing a deeper appreciation for the mysteries that lie beyond our earthly existence.

Here at *The Witches' Almanac* we are proud to bring you a selection of Astrological/astronomical information with each published issue—the celebrity horoscope, eclipses and retrogrades, planting by the Moon, Presage: predictions for the twelve Zodiac signs, the Moon Calendar, sunrise and sunset times and more.

❧ HOLIDAYS ❧

Spring 2024 to Spring 2025

March 20, 2024 . . . . Vernal Equinox
April 1 . . . . All Fools' Day
April 30 . . . . Walpurgis Night
May 1 . . . . Beltane
May 8 . . . . White Lotus Day
May 22 . . . . Vesak Day
May 29 . . . . Oak Apple Day
June 5 . . . . Night of the Watchers
June 20 . . . . Summer Solstice
June 24 . . . . Midsummer
July 23 . . . . Ancient Egyptian New Year
July 31 . . . . Lughnassad Eve
August 1 . . . . Lammas
August 13 . . . . Diana's Day
August 17 . . . . Black Cat Appreciation Day
Setember 6 . . . . Ganesh Chaturthi
September 22 . . . . Autumnal Equinox
October 31 . . . . Samhain Eve
November 1 . . . . Hallowmas
November 16 . . . . Hecate Night
December 16 . . . . Fairy Queen Eve
December 17 . . . . Saturnalia
December 21 . . . . Winter Solstice
January 9, 2025 . . . . Feast of Janus
January 29 . . . . Chinese New Year
February 1 . . . . Oimelc Eve
February 2 . . . . Candlemas
February 15 . . . . Lupercalia
March 1 . . . . Matronalia
March 19 . . . . Minerva's Day

Art Director . . . . Gwion Vran

Astrologer . . . . Dikki-Jo Mullen

Climatologist . . . . Tom C. Lang

Cover Art and Design . . . . Kathryn Sky-Peck

Sales . . . . Roy Singleton

Bookkeeping . . . . D. Lamoureux

Fulfillment . . . . Casey M.

ANDREW THEITIC
Executive Editor

JEAN MARIE WALSH
Associate Editor

MAB BORDEN
Copy Editor

∽ CONTENTS ∾

CONTENTS

Bowl of oak and earthen jar,
Honey of the honey-bee;
Milk of kine and Grecian wine,
Golden corn from neighbouring lea—
These our offerings, Pan, to thee,
Goat-foot god of Arcady.

Horned head and cloven hoof—
Fawns who seek and nymphs that flee—
Piping clear and draweth near
Through the vales of Arcady—
These the gifts we have of thee,
God of joyous ecstasy.

Come, great Pan, and bless us all:
Bless the corn and honey-bee.
Bless the kine and bless the vine,
Bless the vales of Arcady.
Bless the nymphs that laugh and flee,
God of all fertility.

> Sung by Mona Freeman
> *The Goat-Foot God,*
> DION FORTUNE

Yesterday, Today and Tomorrow

by Timi Chasen

EMBALMING 101 Scientists have known that the process of mummification was known in the ancient land of Kemet. The recent discovery of mummification workshops in the necropolis outside of Cairo and in Saqqara indicate that the art of embalming has been in use for more than 4400 years. In fact, the oldest known tomb is for a priest and scribe named Ne Hesut Ba dating to somewhere around 2400 BCE.

Among archeologists it was a common belief that the art of mummification came about as a result of the use of coffins. Most held that the preserved bodies from the old kingdom buried in the ground were naturally embalmed due to the arid conditions of the desert. This has been disproved by recent testing of these remains with results showing that the skin of the bodies had traces of resins and perfumes.

Another discovery of note is that the recipe used for embalming was not standard across Egypt. Geography and social station dictated much about the process used for mummification. The body of a priest or that of a royal line would be treated with natron salt and the finest of resins and perfumes with the body being wrapped in fine linen strips. That of the less fortunate more than likely would not have used the most recent methods or the best of materials.

The cost and scarcity of wood forced many to recycle a coffin. While it was unlikely that embalmers would raid a tomb, they might not be averse to taking coffins from raided tombs. The business of the dead was a lively business indeed in ancient Egypt.

8

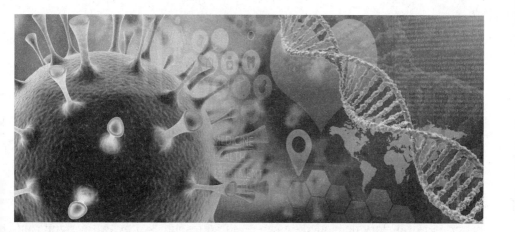

ZOMBIES GO VIRAL Frozen in the permafrost for tens of thousands of years is a veritable horde of viruses that could very well be an existential threat to humans and other animals. Man's technological hastening has all happened in a blip of time compared to what it took for the great apes to evolve into the homo sapiens that we are now. These same advances that have made life easier, if unchecked, will precipitate humanity's demise.

In an effort to gage the viability of frozen viruses, several scientists have taken core samples over a wide range of geographical locations, carefully bringing the samples above freezing level. Cultured single-cell amoebae were exposed to the now-defrosted pathogens, showing that they could indeed infect. With safety in the forefront, scientists used viruses that could only infect single cell-life. In most cases, the scientists used "giant viruses" visible under a microscope.

One fifth of the Northern Hemisphere is covered by permafrost. Because of deep cold and lack of oxygen, these lands act as one large area of preservation of a bounty of life from ancient times. This has allowed scientists to directly study the animal life that has long since become extinct, plant life long gone—the discovery of seeds has allowed scientists to grow plants now extinct—as well as being able to explore the microbial world of yore.

In addition to being the storehouse of ancient life, the permafrost has been the storage ground for many of the cold war byproducts, such as chemicals and radioactive wastes.

Unfortunately the frozen regions of the planet are warming at an unprecedented pace. Scientists are racing to understand the multifaceted impact that the thaw will have on all of humanity and the beings that we share this world with.

9

POWER FROM TREES TO STARS
Humans have been chasing an energy source that is cheap and accessible for millennia. New energy sources were always heralded as being the best and most efficient. Humankind has for the better part of history depended on carbon-based sources of energy.

Initially depending on organic fuels, wood was a primary source of energy throughout the world for thousands of years. Other organic materials such as peat were used where prevalent— interestingly peat is the first step in coal formation. Additionally, in many parts of the world—mountainous regions in Europe and India—caked and dried cow dung is used as fuel.

Water and wind as energy sources were used in limited ways prior to the twentieth century. This passive form of energy was applied in the form of mills. Wind and hydropower turbine wheels were used for grinding wheat. With the advent of electricity, turbines can drive power generation and they provide about sixteen percent of the worlds energy needs.

The Industrial Revolution brought about a shift from wood to fossil fuels such as coal, oil and natural gas. While these resources provided a significant boost to global energy, they also impacted the environment.

Nuclear fission was initially thought to be the savior. Creating immense energy by splitting heavy metal nuclei, nuclear power plants offered a cleaner alternative to fossil fuels. The radioactive waste, however, calls into question its use into the future.

At long last, there are two sources of energy that are completely renewable and it might truly be the saviors of the environment. The first is the use of solar photovoltaic panels that convert solar radiation into electrical energy. Although the fabrication of panels does leave a carbon impact, it is a one-time occurrence. The second, while not really *solar*, is

10

based on the physics of the stars. Fusion reactors aim to replicate the process that powers the Sun merging atomic nuclei, releasing immense amounts of clean energy. The drawback is that the high temperatures necessary to incite fusion requires large amounts of input energy and magnetic confinement of super heated plasma. Scientists have finally been able to contain the plasma and achieve a net gain of energy. Fusion, the energy that powers stars, could provide an abundant, safe and virtually limitless source of energy without greenhouse gas emissions or long-lived radioactive waste.

WHEN IN TUSCANY DO AS THE ETRUSCANS Known for its picturesque vistas, the central Italian region of Tuscany has deep roots that trace back to the Etruscan civilization. The Etruscans were an advanced and influential culture that flourished on the Italian peninsula from the eighth to the third centuries BCE. Known for

their mastery of metalwork and unique artistic style, they left behind a rich archaeological heritage.

Italy's ministry of culture announced the discovery of well-preserved Etruscan figures in Tuscany's San Casciano hot spring mud. The excavation revealed over twenty bronze statues, including Apollo and Hygieia, along with 5,000 coins made of gold, silver and bronze. Before Roman dominance, the Italian peninsula was inhabited by various peoples, including the Etruscans. These statues dating from the second century BCE were created during a period when the Etruscans were gradually assimilated into Roman society. This assimilation followed centuries of territorial warfare.

This find is unique as most surviving Etruscan statues are terracotta. The bronze statues will be exhibited in a new museum located in a sixteenth century building in San Casciano..

11

www.TheWitchesAlmanac.com

 Come visit us at the Witches' Almanac website

12

News from The Witches' Almanac

Glad tidings from the staff

t is that time of the year when the culmination of our year-long efforts begins to bear ruit. The creation of the annual edition of *The Witches' Almanac* has always been, nd will always be, an act of love. In this endeavor we respond to a powerful call o action, emphasizing the significance of active participation and engagement with he diverse and varied voices within our community. We are reminded that it is both privilege and a responsibility to provide a platform where these voices can freely nform, impart, share and even provoke.

This year our chosen theme is "Fire: Forging Freedom." What better way to omprehend freedom than through the words and thoughts that ignite the soul and nspire it to soar? As we find ourselves on the eve of tomorrow, we persevere and trive for that freedom not only for ourselves but for all.

We are thrilled to announce the introduction of *Ancient Holidays*, an exciting new ook series that delves into the spiritual calendars of ancient civilizations. As we wrap p this year's *Almanac*, we are also adding the finishing touches to the inaugural three ooks in this series and will shortly begin on the fourth. Authored by our very own Mab Borden, these books offer profound and insightful explorations of the calendars ollowed by the ancient Egyptians, Greeks, and Romans. We are confident that this eries will not only provide valuable information but also ignite inspiration for our piritual observations.

In *The Witches' Almanac* Issue 43, we present an exciting collection of brilliant minds, eaturing a mix of familiar and up-and-coming thinkers within our community. We varmly welcome Jack Chanek, Sali Crow, Heather Greene, Lucius and Leslie Soule to ur pages. *The Witches' Almanac* Issue 43 is historic as it the first edition of the Almanac o be translated into Spanish! Additionally, we proudly introduce the *2024 Witches' Almanac Wall Calendar*, centered around the theme of Gods from around the world. As lways, you can anticipate captivating imagery and concise explanations of each deity.

We strive to enhance your experience at TheWitchesAlmanac.com, our online store nd Pagan resource center. Here are some important updates: early editions of *The Witches' Almanac* are running out. Grab them before they're gone as they won't be vailable for long. Many of Atramentous' exquisite books are becoming sought-after ollector's items, as they won't be reprinted. *Welsh Witches: Narratives of Witchcraft and Magic from 16th and 17th Century Wales* is already sold out in the UK and our stock s running low. The *50 Year Anniversary Edition of The Witches' Almanac* and *Magic: n Occult Primer—50 Year Anniversary Edition* are highly favored by our shoppers. hey've become must-haves and continue to be in high demand. Will there be reprints? Only time will tell!

13

When Folk Art Becomes Folk Magic

*On the development of Pennsylvania Dutch Hex Signs,
Fraktur and Magical folk arts*

SOMETIMES ART is simply for art's sake, sometimes art records history, and sometimes art becomes magic! In fact, in preliterate societies art was sometimes considered an act of magic and developing later into a means of communication as well as medium of expression. In the course of time, art and magic shared a two way street, wherein folk art developed from magic and magical art seeped into culture, becoming folk art.

A fine example of this interchange between magical art, folk art and art as a medium of communication can found in the Northern European societies of the Teutonic tribes and as we shall see, their descendants that later came to North America. As is the case for many cultures, the writing system that was loosely used by the Proto-Germanic—Elder Futhark—had magical uses that reached well beyond simple communication. Each symbol

in the alphabet represents both a sound and a mundane/magical property.

While historians are unsure which came first, the mundane or the magical use of Elder Futhark, it is quite evident that its magical use was quite prevalent. The use of Futhark on jewelry was common—with time. Various letters of Futhark were combined in an artistic manner to produce a desired protection or blessing. The user would be aware of the occult nature of the jewelry.

The custom of combining letters of the Futhark in a utilitarian manner that has artistic appeal is still practiced by some citizens of Iceland. The magical charms known as *galdrastafir* (magical staves) are aesthetically appealing while being employed for a very magical purpose. For a deep dive into the galdrastafir practiced in Iceland, *Icelandic Magic: Practical Secrets of the Northern Grimoires* is an excellent

place to start. In it is a treasure trove of detailed drawings of the various charms.

It is not uncommon to find various runes that were incorporated into building structures. The popular post and beam construction—known as *holzfachwerk* in Germany, *half-timbering* by the English—was decorative as well as utilitarian. The angular beam structures were easily adapted to allow for runes to be incorporated into both the interior and exterior construction. While this style of construction and the inclusion of magical symbols is evident in early Germanic structures, its popularity rose in fifteenth century. The house in the above image has a number of runes incorporated into the architecture.

Quilting and needlework are art forms that have been practiced globally for as almost as long as recorded history, if not longer. While it is unclear when they arrived in Teutonic societies, there has

been a strong connection with quilting as folk art and indirectly as magic among the Germanic peoples for quite some time. Needless to say, the very utilitarian arts of quilting and needlework easily lent themselves to being crossover media whereby folk magic could be expressed.

The emigrating Germanic peoples of the 1600s who would become the Pennsylvania Dutch (Deutch) brought all of the above-mentioned folk arts and folk beliefs with them. They found fertile ground to continue to grow and even change as they mixed with the many ethnicities that they encountered.

The two most recognizable folk art forms are Fraktur and Hex Signs. These two art forms are easily recognized by tourists and collectors alike as epitomizing the domestic folk arts of the various groups of Pennsylvania Dutch. In fact, all discussion regarding folk art and subsequently folk magic in Pennsylvania would be incomplete without these two art forms and the impact that they had on each other.

Deriving its name from the black letter calligraphic lettering native to German speaking northern Europe, Fraktur consists of an illuminated folk art that is specific to the Pennsylvania Dutch. Like other illuminated manuscripts, Fraktur are hand drawn documents which were used almost exclusively to record life events, the majority of which were experienced in a religious context. These included but were not limited to births, baptisms and marriages. As this art form evolved, its use expanded into marking achievements in school such as exemplary scholastic ability and graduation. As the expansion

into mundane uses ensued, Fraktur also developed into an art form where a blessing was bestowed on a person or a new household or for spiritual upliftment, illuminating quotes from the Bible.

There is a scholarly debate whether the motifs employed in Fraktur are simply embellishing art or if they are iconography. While one could argue the case of both, the argument should include examining similar trends in Fraktur's European antecedents, which did tend towards iconography. The folk art employed on Fraktur clearly connects with communal understanding of the symbolic meaning behind the art. A rose was not simply a rose—it held the mystery of mystical transcendence. The *distelfink* (a stylized

The Symbol	Its Meaning
Circle	Eternity or infinity
Distelfink (Bird)	Good luck and happiness
Dove	Peace and contentment
Eagle	Good health, strength and courage
Four-Pointed Star	Bright day
Heart	Love and kindness
Horse Head	Protect animals from disease & buildings from lightning
Maple Leaf	Contentment
Oak Leaf	Strength
Quarter Moons (4)	Four seasons of the year
Raindrops	Abundance, fertility, rain
Rosette	Good luck, keep away bad luck and evil
Star	Good luck
Triple Star	Success, wealth and happiness
Tulip	Faith
Tulips (Trinity—3)	Faith, hope and charity
Twelve-Pointed Rosette	A joyous month for each month of the year
Unicorn	Virtue and piety—belief in God
Wavy Border	Smooth sailing through life

gold finch) imbued the art with a blessing of good luck and happiness. This was a code that most of the Deutch of Pennsylvania understood.

Directly related to Fraktur are the Hex signs that have become commercially extant in the twentieth century. Like Fraktur they may have had a humble beginning as simple signs of artistic or talismanic importance painted on barns, they have evolved in sophistication as both folk art and a magical art form.

The etymology of the word Hex is certainly debated. Some believe that is taken from the German meaning of "hex." Others believe that it may originate from the attribution of hex being a six pointed object—stars of varying points appear in many Hex signs.

Alpine Germans have a rich history of artwork that is similar to the Hex signs of Pennsylvania Dutch artwork. Some of the symbols are believed to be pre-Christian remnants of Germanic

society. For example, a circled rosette is called the Sun of the Alps. While there isn't conclusive proof, it is not beyond the pale to believe as much.

Whether by fancy or fact, Zook was instrumental in the spread Hex popularity. He believed that Hex signs were more than just art, they had meaning and were possibly meant to be talismanic. His Jacob Zook's Family Crafts disseminated Hex signs widely. He would later write *Hexology: The History and Meanings of Hex Symbols* that in many ways codified the symbols and made popular the numerous venues that began to distribute Hex signs to tourists.

Hex signs are the perfect example of the evolution of folk art to folk magic. The craft of the hexmeister is only limited by ability and imagination. On the previous page, is a list of the common symbols used in Hexology. Let the magic begin!

−DEVON STRONG

17

The Real Wonders of the Ancient World

MOST PEOPLE have heard of the classical Seven Wonders of the Ancient World even if they are not really familiar with what exactly they were. These were the Hellenistic wonders, recorded over two thousand years ago by an ancient Greek historian named Antipater of Sidon whose world generally encompassed the area surrounding the Mediterranean Sea.

The most ancient of the wonders was the Great Pyramid of Giza—the construction and mathematics of the Giza Complex are truly astounding! To the East were the Hanging Gardens of Babylon, located in what is now Iraq and which were built around 600 BCE. This was a multistory garden complete with plants and trees from around all the lands known at that time. It was built by King Nebuchadnezzar II for his wife Amytis, who missed the lush vegetation of Persia. One of its noted features was the sophisticated irrigation system built to water the above-grade vegetation.

Two wonders were on the Turkish coast. First was the Greek temple of Artemis at Ephesus, built in 541 BCE. The enormous structure was 430 feet long by 60 feet wide with 127 marble columns! It was built to honor Artemis, the Greek Goddess who presided over the hunt, wilderness, childbirth and chastity. At Ephesus the statue of Artemis was adorned with many breasts, symbolizing her care of children. A hundred miles to the South was another wonder—the Mausoleum at Halicarnassus. Built around 350 BCE for the Persian king Mausolus and his wife Artemisia II of Caria, it is one of the very few wonders that still survives in some form. This burial structure was ornate and five sculptors were hired to create different portions of it! King Mausolus gave his name to a type of building in his honor and his building was used as a model in the neoclassical period.

A ferry can take you from Halicarnassus just ninety miles South to the Greek island of Rhodes to the

18

site of another wonder. In ancient times, you'd have seen it from the deck before landing—the famous Colossus of Rhodes built in 292 BCE. Roughly the same height and proportion as the Statue of Liberty in New York Harbor, this statue of Helios was built in bronze over an iron frame, stood on a large pedestal, possibly held up an arm used as a light and was adorned with a crown of solar rays. The colossal statue was rather short lived, however, as it fell to the ground during an earthquake in 226 BCE. Offers to rebuild it were rejected by the Rhodians because an oracle had warned against it. In mainland Greece the statue of Zeus at Olympia—a forty foot high seated figure—was housed within a building not tall enough for him to stand. Zeus was a chryselephantine statue, meaning he was constructed of ivory over wood and gold-plated bronze. This wonder was built around 435 BCE and may have survived until 425 CE when the temple housing it burned.

Returning to Egypt, the final wonder of the ancient world was the Lighthouse of Alexandria. Built around 260 BCE, this magnificent lighthouse used a series of polished metal mirrors to guide mariners several miles out at sea. These mirrors—placed at the top of the structure which stood more than three hundred feet—were mainly used in the daytime as nocturnal maritime navigation was not frequent at the time. Fires could be lit in the base of the structure and reflected upwards to the main mirror for nighttime use, however. It possibly also employed a dumbwaiter type of system to haul firewood up to the top. The lighthouse

Seated Zeus in Athens

stood until 1375 CE, when its materials were reused to construct a fortress.

While these seven structures were certainly noteworthy, there are far more wondrous feats of artistry to be found all over the entire world and many are much older. A brief explanation of some of these wonders will hopefully entice the reader to begin further research and embark on a fascinating journey into the ancient world. Beginning again with the Great Pyramid of Giza, a more thorough list includes all of the incredibly ancient remains of the Egyptian civilization. To describe these remains briefly is

19

impossible—it would fill a library! The best way to begin to grasp the antiquity of the Sphinx, the complexity of the Dendera Temple or the ceiling in the Temple of Hathor is to see them.

The Americas

Turning to another corner of the globe, the Yucatan Peninsula in Mexico is loaded with ruins, and is a popular tourist site to begin exploring. With many similarities to the Giza plateau, the Pyramid of the Sun in Teotihuacan, Mexico is part of a complex ancient city on the outskirts of modern Mexico City. This pyramid—with many layers built over the previous incarnations—was originally built above an ancient cave. It lies adjacent to the Pyramid of the Moon as well as several other smaller structures and it appears to be above many unexplored ruins visible with ground penetrating radar and other new technology. These structures were aligned to observe certain solar and lunar events.

The incredible pyramids and ornate ruins of Central and South America are worthy of attention. The lost empires of the Toltec, Olmec, Inca, Aztec and Maya civilizations left very ancient and extremely sophisticated ruins all throughout Central and South America, with the level of magnificence rising the further back in time you travel. Massive megalithic stones whose joinery seems to be melted into place with each multisided block are found on the lowest, most ancient portions of the structures. These elements are seen in other parts of the globe around the same timeframe and are usually referred to as cyclopean construction— an adage referring to the mythical giant race of cyclopes who would be able to lift the stone blocks. Other major sites in this area include Copan in Honduras, Tikal in Guatemala and Caracol in Belize. In South America, Tiwanaku and Puma Punku in Bolivia are easily wonders of their own. Puma Punku features perfectly milled megalithic blocks that appear to have been part of a fortress or wall, but there is little explanation as to how they were made. The site was most likely built by the Tiwanaku people and subsequently was reused by the Inca.

About four hundred miles North of Puma Punku, the Lost City of the Incas can be found atop mount Machu Picchu, 7,970 feet above sea level. Again, cyclopean construction can be seen in this remote city with the oldest foundation blocks being much larger and more refined than the medium (but still huge and expertly crafted) blocks built at a later time above them and the smaller, unrefined newer blocks at the top, placed by more modern cultures. These older blocks are joined so closely together as to seem as though they were somehow softened and pushed together like clay. But they are hard granite, thousands of feet up a mountaintop! What magic could

20

have been at play to help form them?

India is rich with megalithic and extremely ornately carved stone temples. There are thousands of temples throughout the Indian subcontinent—some extremely ancient and in ruins and others used in daily prayers to this day. The Meenakshi Temple in Madurai, Tamil Nadu is a Dravidian example of a modern temple complex. The Ellora Caves are a series of over a hundred caves that have been carved out of hard basalt for Hindu, Buddhist and Jain temples. The seventeen Hindu caves include the Kailasa Temple, which is a multistory masterpiece carved out of solid rock that easily rivals European cathedrals built from comparatively small blocks of stone. The engineering and skill required to sculpt a structure of this magnitude—complete with ornate decorative artwork—is difficult to conceive. This was a temple dedicated to Shiva and is certainly fit for a God! The twelve Buddhist caves are somewhat simpler in ornamentation but are still comparable

to large, three-story monastery buildings perfectly cut into solid basalt cliffs. Cave ten is the exception as it features a round, vaulted ceiling with an organic appearance. Many large carvings of Gautama Buddha, bodhisattvas and saints are included in the shrines. Finally, the five Jain caves feature poetry carved in stone.

Asia and Oceania

Moving East, the Ankor Wat in Cambodia is a city and temple complex built of stone. The massive structures with numerous stone faces are surrounded by similar temple cities also built by the Khmer. Angkor Thom is close by and the temple Ta Phrom has been untouched for centuries with jungle growth reclaiming portions of the ancient carved stonework. These are truly wonders of human creation, sharing the lush green vegetation in a symbiosis with nature.

In China, a truly massive group of caves called the Xiaonanhai Stone Chambers or the Longyou Caves were discovered in Zhejiang province

Machu Picchu

21

Angkor Wat

in 1992. These twenty-four artificial sandstone caverns have heights of 98 feet, with the total area—perfectly excavated—being 320,000 square feet, for purposes unknown.

Located in the Pacific Ocean, Easter Island is home to the many large statues called Moai. These were carved from volcanic rock by the Rapa Nui people and range in size up to 33 feet tall. Hundreds of these statues were quarried, shaped, transported to remote locations and set into place to overlook the ocean. Some have been found to include full bodies—they were buried up to their chests but were fully detailed and protected by the elements while in the island soil.

A very strange structure called Nan Madol is found on the Island of Pohnpei—part of Micronesia in the Pacific Ocean, East of Papua New Guinea. This structure or walled fortress was constructed of columns of basalt stone, much like a massive stone log cabin. Who built this in the middle of the Pacific Ocean, when and why is a mystery which has given rise to many local myths. The intrigue grows with legends that it could be part of the lost continent of Mu or Lemuria, as written by James Churchward in 1926.

Europe and Africa

In Cappadocia in Turkey a number of sprawling caves and tunnels form an ancient underground city. This network is complete with animal stables, numerous airshafts, defensive areas and trap doors, all connected on multiple levels. The Church of Saint George in Lalibela, Ethiopia is another megalithic structure sculpted out of solid bedrock, similar to those found in India. This several-story building was cut below grade and forms the shape of an equal-armed cross standing in a perfectly excavated hollow in the stone. The construction is once again cyclopean and shows what appears to be a softening of the stone where it was sculpted like clay, although no techniques are known that would explain how this was done.

Truly massive megalithic remains are seen all over the globe, which would be nearly or actually impossible to construct or move using today's technology. In Lebanon the Baalbek Stones are among the largest ever quarried by humans. Named for the Temple of Jupiter Baal, the largest of these monolithic blocks is estimated at 1,650 tons. These stones include the Stone of the Pregnant Woman, Stone of the South, the Forgotten Stone and the Trilithon—a group of placed stones which possibly once formed the base of the Temple of Jupiter Baal. Each measures around sixty-two feet long, thirteen feet high and twelve feet thick with weights of 750-800 tons individually!

Heading into further remote times, dolmens are unique stone structures resembling Fred Flintstone houses. These tombs were constructed either by perfectly hollowing out a solid block of granite, or by placing large, flat granite components together to form an enormously heavy house of cards. A single hole forms the doorway, with some retaining their round, solid granite plug-like door. Dolmens can be found in many locations but are especially common in Northern Europe and the Korean Peninsula.

Turning to a very strange megalithic ruin, the extremely deep, shaft-like cave excavated by an unknown group of people in Kebardino-Balkaria in Russia seems truly otherworldly. This vertical shaft was precisely cut into granite and extends down hundreds if not thousands of feet. The shaft makes several right angles before extending down along the same axis again, almost as though it is a trap or mechanism to deter things from falling straight down to the seemingly bottomless depths. It is truly unique.

To bring this journey to a close, consider that the classical Wonders of the World are magnificent but very narrow in focus—there is so much that is more wonderous and unknown. Perhaps even some of the natural landforms that are usually taken for granted were once part of something grander and represent the remnants of long-lost civilizations completely forgotten by the modern world, remaining in such ruin and decay as to render them invisible to the unsuspecting eye. It seems that the further back you go, the more grand and mysterious the wonders of the world become.

—JOHN N

Lalibela Church in Ethiopia

DIVINE POWER TO HEAL OR HARM

Sacred Venom

*"Within all good (light, life) is evil (darkness, death)
and within all evil (darkness, death) is good (light, life.)"*

ALL THINGS contain their opposites—death holds life and life death, good holds evil and evil good, light holds darkness and darkness holds light. The idea that the roles in the magical universe of good and evil are each a part of the same universal whole is expressed globally in numerous spiritual and magical traditions. In the Far East the yin and yang symbol illustrates this concept. A circle divided into equal portions of dark (yin) and light (yang) with a dot of white within the black side and a corresponding dot of black embedded in the white half shows how the polarities embrace each other.

Among the pantheon of Pagan deities, sacred powers that both heal and harm are present to support this recurring theme. Intriguingly, venoms can be deadly yet they have life saving capabilities and can be a tool of the Gods and Goddesses. Tarantulas are an example. There are over

800 species of these large, hairy, befanged spiders found all over the world. Many come from the Mediterranean region as well as Mexico and South America. Tarantulas are sold in pet stores, usually priced from about $20 to $200, depending upon their size and rarity. They are carnivores, thriving on a diet of insects and can be found living happily in the humid environments of home terrariums. Witches throughout the ages have selected them as familiars.

Spiders are connected with magical and divine powers in many God and Goddess traditions. Maya, a Hindu deity associated with illusions, is one. Her spider weaves a sacred web that provides invisibility. Native American legends present a spider totem to invoke for maintaining balance in the world. In Lady Wilde's 1877 reference book *Ancient Legends, Mystic Charms and Superstitions of Ireland,* spiders are linked

with sacred looms, wheels and gossamer, a thread used by faeries for weaving. Celtic beliefs also regarded spiders with awe as their webs could be gathered and used as a life-saving compress to stop excessive bleeding. In the Torah spiders saved the life of David when he hid in a cave from the soldiers of Saul and spiders spun a huge web across the entrance. This led the soldiers to turn away, thinking that no one could be inside because the web blocked the entrance.

Several Native American cultures have creation stories revolving around sacred spider stories as well. There is a Pima tribal teaching about a huge spider web stretched across the void to create the Earth. The Pima are Native Americans from Arizona and they trace their ancestry back to the Hohokam people who originated from the Aztecs. In the Central and Southern coastal regions of California are the Chumash, whose storytellers have another sacred spider creation tradition. This involves the daily journey of the Sun God who rests in a hole created for him by Spider Woman. Cave paintings found in California depict this divine link.

Today scientists recognize the divine and lifegiving powers of spiders in the venom milked from tarantulas. The venom contains a peptide toxin identified as ProTxII. Forget aspirin! This venom can be processed to make a medicine to ease headaches, backaches and other bodily discomforts. Although venomous bites from tarantulas are rarely fatal, they can cause blurry vision, tremors and fainting spells. A skin irritation can occur with a tarantula bite also but this is actually caused by irritation from the creatures' bristle-like hairs which are

similar to stinging nettles. Injuries of this kind are called urticating stings.

In the 14th century in Italy, field workers who were frequently bitten by tarantulas developed a sacred dance with the intent to rid themselves of the Old Mother Tarantula. This folk dance is called the tarantella, the dance of the spider. It originated in the small town of Taranto. It was believed that dancing in a frenzy until exhausted into a collapse would drive out and cancel the evil and deadly effects of the bite. Special musicians would play a musical accompaniment with tambourines, mandolins, and guitars while the victim completed the lifesaving holy dance. Today the tarantella dance survives as a social event—it is considered bad luck to dance it alone. Dancers present the tarantella as an entertaining performance. Often they wear red, green and white outfits to match the colors of the Italian flag.

—GRANIA LING

25

Modern Superstitions About Sneezing

excerpted from The Magic of the Horseshoe with Other Folk Lore Notes *by Robert Means Lawrence (1898)*

SNEEZING at the commencement of an undertaking, whether it be an important enterprise or the most commonplace act, has usually been accounted unlucky. Thus, according to a modern Teutonic belief, if a man sneeze on getting up in the morning, he should lie down again for another three hours, else his wife will be his master for a week. So likewise the pious Hindu, who may perchance sneeze while beginning his morning ablutions in the river Ganges, immediately recommences his prayers and toilet; and among the Alfoorans or aborigines of the island of Celebes in the Indian archipelago, if one happens to sneeze when about leaving a gathering of friends, he at once resumes his seat for a while before making another start.

When a native of the Banks Islands, in Polynesia, sneezes, he imagines that some one is calling his name, either with good or evil intent, the motive being shown by the character of the sneeze. Thus a gentle sneeze implies kindly feeling on the part of the person speaking of him, while a violent paroxysm indicates a malediction.

In the latter case he resorts to a peculiar form of divination in order to ascertain who it is that curses him. This consists in raising the arms above the head and revolving the closed fists one around the other. The revolution of the fists is the question, "Is it such an one?" Then the arms are thrown out, and the answer, presumably affirmative, is given by the cracking of the elbow-joints.

In Scotland even educated people have been known to maintain that idiots are incapable of sneezing, and hence, if this be true, the inference is clear that the act of sternutation is *prima facie* evidence of the possession of a certain degree of intelligence.

British nurses used to think that infants were under a fairy spell until they sneezed. "God sain the bairn," exclaimed an old Scotch nurse when her little charge sneezed at length, "it's no a warlock."

The Irish people also entertain similar beliefs. Thus in Lady Wilde's "Ancient Cures, Charms, and Usages of Ireland" (p. 41) is to be found the

following description of a magical ceremony for the cure of a fairy-stricken child. A good fire is made, wherein is thrown a quantity of certain herbs prescribed by the fairy women; and after a thick smoke has risen, the child is carried thrice around the fire while an incantation is repeated and holy water is sprinkled about liberally. Meantime all doors must be closed, lest some inquisitive fairy enter and spy upon the proceedings; and the magical rites must be continued *until the child sneezes three times*, for this looses the spell, and the little one is permanently redeemed from the power of witches.

Among uncivilized peoples the sneeze of a young child has a certain mystic significance, and is intimately

associated with its prospective welfare or ill-luck. When, therefore, a Maori infant sneezes, its mother immediately recites a long charm of words. If the sneeze occurs during a meal, it is thought to be prognostic of a visit, or of some interesting piece of news; whereas in Tonga it is deemed an evil token.

So, too, among the New Zealanders, if a child sneeze on the occasion of receiving its name, the officiating priest at once holds to its ear the wooden image of an idol and sings some mystic words.

In a note appended to his "Mountain Bard," the Ettrick Shepherd says, regarding the superstitions of Selkirkshire: "When they sneeze in first stepping out of bed in the morning, they are thence certified that strangers will be there in the course of the day, in numbers corresponding to the times they sneeze."

It was a Flemish belief that a sneeze during a conversation proved that what one said was the truth, a doctrine which must have commended itself to snuff-takers.

In Shetlandic and Welsh folk-lore the sneeze of a cat indicates cold north winds in summer and snow in winter; and the Bohemians have an alleged infallible test for recognizing the Devil, for they believe that he must perforce sneeze violently at sight of a cross.

According to a Chinese superstition a sneeze on New Year's Eve is ominous for the coming year; and, to offset this, the sneezer must visit three families of different surnames, and beg from each a small tortoise-shaped cake, which must be eaten before midnight.

In Turkistan, when a person to whom a remark is addressed sneezes, it is an asseveration that the opinion or statement is correct, just as if the person accosted were to exclaim, "That is true!" In the same country three sneezes are unlucky. When, also, any one hiccoughs, it is etiquette to say, "You stole something from me," and this phrase at such times is supposed to produce good luck.

The Japanese attach significance to the number of times a man sneezes. Thus, one sneeze indicates that some one is praising him, while two betoken censure or disparagement; a triple sneeze is commonplace, and means simply that a person has taken cold. In Mexico, also, it was formerly believed either that somebody was speaking evil of one who sneezed, or that he was being talked about by one or more persons.

Sussex people are prejudiced against cats which develop sneezing proclivities, for they believe that, when a pet feline sneezes thrice, it augurs ill for the health of the household, and is premonitory of influenza and bronchial affections.

In an interesting article in "Macmillan's Magazine," entitled "From the Note-book of a Country Doctor," a physician practicing in a remote part of Cornwall tells of a peculiar cure for deafness which recently came to his notice.

One of his patients, an elderly woman whose name was Grace Rickard, complained that she could no longer hear the grunting of her pigs, a sound which, from childhood, had roused her from sleep in the early morning. The doctor was obliged to tell her that the difficulty was due to advancing years.

A short time after, on calling at her house, he found her sitting before the fire with a piece of board in her lap, and deeply absorbed in thought. Just as the door opened, she exclaimed: "Lord, deliver me from my sins," and this petition was followed by a peculiar noise which sounded like an abortive sneeze. "Don't be frited, zur," she said, "'tes aunly a sneeze." "It's the oddest sneeze I ever heard," said the doctor; "why can't you sneeze in the ordinary way?" "So I do, when I can," she explained; "but now 'tes got up to nine times running, and wherever to get nine sneezes from is moor 'n I knaw."

It appeared that Grace was making trial of an infallible cure for deafness, the necessary apparatus for which consisted of a piece of board and some stout pins. One of the latter is stuck into the board every morning, the patient's forefingers being crossed over the pin, while the pious ejaculation above mentioned is repeated simultaneously with a vigorous sneeze. On the next morning two pins must be stuck in the board, the petition and sneeze being once repeated; on the following morning three pins, three prayers, and three sneezes, and so on up to nine times.

—ROBERT MEANS LAWRENCE (1898)

29

The Tiger and the Frog

A Himalayan Tale

It is but seldom tigers leave their natural haunts, or frogs theirs; the tiger his warm jungle, and the frog his home in the swamp. However, they do, and here follows a story of a tiger and a frog who both wandered very far from their homes. The home of the Tiger was in Nepal, and that of the Frog in Tibet. As for the Frog, he was curious, that was all.

In a certain place where the two countries border on one another, the Tiger had found a pool, and he had a long drink, for he was very thirsty. The Frog happened to be hopping near by and saw the Tiger drinking, and the Tiger, looking up, saw the Frog. The curiosity of the Frog led him to hop to the pool, and he too had a drink. When he swallowed the water, he felt a tickling in his throat.

"Hullo!" said the Tiger. "Who are you?"

"I am a frog," replied the Frog, and he asked the Tiger who he was.

The Tiger said, "I am a tiger."

The Frog had heard tell of tigers, and he anxiously inquired of the Tiger what he ate.

"Frogs," replied the Tiger, promptly opening his large jaws and showing a double row of grinders. "Frogs are most succulent. Yes, I eat frogs."

On hearing this the Frog felt alarmed and wished he had remained at home. However, the Tiger could have caught him in one fell swoop if he had attempted to hop away, so he said quickly, "That is strange, because I eat tigers."

On hearing this the Tiger roared with laughter till his great sides shook.

"If," continued the Frog, "you truly eat frogs, prove it to me. Return what you have eaten, because I find it difficult to believe."

"Certainly," said the Tiger, "if you will do the same, for your story is even more difficult to believe."

"I will," said the Frog, who knew that it was the Tiger's hair that was tickling in his throat. "Nothing could be easier than to prove the truth of what I have told you."

The Tiger thereupon brought up some grass, but the Frog with one cough brought up Tiger's hair.

"There you are," said the Frog. But the Tiger didn't wait to hear any more. He turned tail and bolted and left the Frog to compliment himself on the success of his ruse.

Being a wise frog, he hopped back as quickly as he knew how to his homeland swamp to boast to his friends of how he had outwitted a tiger and saved his own skin.

As for the Tiger, he ran quicker than he had ever run before in his life. He was still running when a jackal crossed his path.

"Hi, Tiger!" called the Jackal. "What's your haste? You run as if a devil was after you."

"A devil," panted the Tiger, slowing down. "Worse that that. Over yonder in Tibet I met a frog who eats tigers."

"A frog who eats tigers!" exclaimed the Jackal. "That is absurd. Come, tie your whiskers to mine, and together we will go back and have a look at the curious monster."

"No, no," said the Tiger, quaking. But the Jackal said, "Tiger, what a coward you are," and insisted they should turn back.

So the Tiger and the Jackal knitted their whiskers together and went back. After awhile they came to the swamp where the Frog lived. The Frog was squatting on a stone sunning himself when the Tiger and the Jackal made their appearance.

"Ho," said the Frog, who had told his story so often that he really believed he could eat a tiger. "Ho, so I see you have come back to be eaten, Tiger."

"There! What did I tell you?" said the Tiger to the Jackal. And he turned back and fled, dragging the poor Jackal after him. The Tiger ran and ran, and the Jackal, who could not run so fast got more and more breathless, until all the breath left his body, and he died.

The Tiger, feeling the dead weight of the Jackal, thought, "Ah, he is trying to drag me back. He is in league with the Frog."

"Untie my whiskers," commanded the Tiger. There was no answer. "Untie my whiskers." Still no answer. "Take that," said the Tiger, half turning, and he gave the Jackal a clout on the ear.

The Jackal, who was now rigid, rocked stiffly.

"Hump!" and the Tiger. So you thought you would take me to the Frog to be eaten, and he gave the Jackal another good whack and proceeded to lecture him.

"Yes," went on the Tiger. "You thought you could bind me fast, tying your whiskers to mine, so that I would stand there to be eaten by the Frog, you treacherous beast. Take *that*—and *that*," and he gave the Jackal a few more clouts.

The Jackal rocked and fell sideways.

"To suffer the indignity of being eaten by a frog," and the Tiger wrenched his whiskers free from the Jackal's.

The Jackal lay stiff and stark on the road. The Tiger noticed an unpleasant odor. "The devil's entered into him, and he pretends to be asleep," thought the Tiger, whose nerves were on edge.

Freed from the Jackal, he ran faster yet. Presently he met a tortoise. The Tortoise called: "What makes you run so fast, Tiger?" The Tiger stopped to tell him.

"I've left a jackal over there," said he, "who has a devil in him. A treacherous rascal who tried to get me devoured by a frog."

"Where?" inquired the Tortoise. "Let me have a look at him."

"Not I," said the Tiger, and went into a swoon.

The Tortoise crawled to where the poor Jackal lay and perceived that the Jackal was dead. "What a fool of a tiger," thought the Tortoise, and he gave the Jackal a decent burial.

"A tiger who is afraid of a dead jackal and a harmless frog. A fine lord of beasts—let him remain in a swoon," and the Tortoise gave a sniff and slid into the water.

32

Witchery and The World of Dreams
Touring Inner Space

A GOOD night's sleep is crucial to maintaining both mental and physical health. Sleep disorders are on the rise, perhaps linked to the stresses, food choices and other factors which are a part of modern life. Gaining insight by analyzing dreams and awakening refreshed and rested are the goals of enhancing the potentials of sleep and dream time.

The bizarre and mysterious world of dreams has tantalized and mystified people for thousands of years. References to messages received in dreams are found in early religious texts as well as poems and stories. Even the hieroglyphic records of the ancient Egyptians contain accounts of dreams. Dreams are a key to inner space, and the inner universe you access each time you sleep is where you spend about a third of your life!

Dreams are vital to physical and emotional wellbeing. Experiments show that dream deprivation leads to the development of many undesirable symptoms such as depression and paranoia. In early times, Witches and shamans deliberately guided dream themes to aid in the evolution of those on the spiritual path. Incense burned upon retiring for the night as well as the use of herb-stuffed dream pillows were techniques used to enhance and magnify the dreamscape.

European dream lore is ancient and varied. The second century A.D. writer Artemidoras compiled the very first dream book. He wrote that dreams are infused into people for their advantage and instruction. Eastern European mysticism refers to a doppelganger, a German word meaning body double which was the shadow self, the animal nature which we control by day goes wild at night. This gave rise to tales of werewolves and Jekyll and Hyde

33

legends linked to the dream state. A focus on dreams opens a whole new perception of the self.

Psychologists Sigmund Freud and Carl Jung are credited with overcoming the deceptively casual attitudes people had toward dreams at the end of the nineteenth and in the early part of the twentieth centuries. Today, society has come full circle in dream work. Once again recording dreams for future reference and dwelling upon a theme in hopes of exploring it in the dream state are common practices. Recurring dreams, shared dreams, precognitive dreams, communication with the spirit world and nightmares are all variations on the dream experience.

The study of dreams is both practical and informative. Some guidelines for starting involve being aware of common themes experienced in dreams. These are:

Food theme dreams: these relate to desires and appetites which seek to be satisfied. Food dreams can be a metaphor for money and power as well as fulfillment in love.

Flying: flight in dreams can show an urge to escape, to get ahead or to move on a spiritual quest to a higher level.

Prophetic and preparatory dreams: these describe events to come and are the mind's way of getting ready for the future.

A dream uninterpreted is like a letter unread. There's a tremendous reservoir of comfort and healing to be found in working with dreams. Begin by keeping a journal, either in writing or on tape. In time it will become easier to recall more detail as you become accustomed to recording dreams each day. Even for those who

say they don't dream or recall dreams ever, just writing down a single word or lingering emotion will soon bring about a whole new level of insight. It's important to make a record of dreams immediately upon waking. Once the feet touch the floor we are grounded in the everyday waking world and the dreams fade, so it's best to do dream work while still lying in bed.

Herbal preparations as well as crystals are marvelous resources which have been used by Witches for generations. Some herbs assist with bringing a deep, restful sleep while others are better for dream recall. Experimenting with combinations of sleep and dream herbs is an easy way to customize one's own sleep and dream time. A simple rule of thumb recipe for brewing a dream tea is to add a heaping teaspoon of dried herbs to eight ounces—a standard cup—of boiling water. Allow this to sit for about five minutes, then strain and sip. Add lemon and sweetener as desired. For iced tea, add extra herbs, increase the wait time and add ice. Drinks made with fresh herbs are called tisanes and require a larger amount of the leaves, flowers or roots. Tisanes are a little more difficult to prepare but they do offer the additional advantage of adding fresh minerals, vitamins and enzymes.

Herbs for Sleep and Dreams

Rosemary to deepen sleep while controlling disturbing dreams and night terrors.

Catnip brings a relaxing and deep sleep.

34

Mugwort will enhance dream recall and generate lucid dreams.

Hops for inner peace and release from the painful memories, disappointments or anger which can disturb sleep.

Lavender for calming and soothing while treating headaches.

Chamomile served as a traditional nursery tea to calm children of all ages and promote a peaceful, dreamless sleep.

Cloves overcomes chills and brings vivid, creative dreams (use sparingly, just one, two or three cloves per cup).

Spearmint for clear and vivid, easily remembered and easy-to-interpret dreams.

Peppermint called the aspirin of the herb world, peppermint is a favorite overall tonic to relieve weariness, vague aches and pains and general malaise.

As an alternative to brewing the suggested herbs as a tea they can also be gathered into a small bag to use as a dream sachet pillow for aromatherapy. Use about three tablespoons of dried herbs. Add a few drops of essential oil— lavender or peppermint are excellent choices—for extra fragrance. Sleep next to the dream sachet or suspend it over your bed, perhaps attached to a dream catcher.

Crystals for Sleep and Dreams

Crystals can be added to a dream sachet, worn as a ring or pendant or assembled in a medicine bag to hold or suspend above the bed. These are popular choices.

Malachite aids dream interpretation and relieves nightmares.

Herkimer Diamond or Clear Quartz amplifies and clarifies dreams

Chrysoprase brings a sense of protection and security, relieves nightmares and brings safety from sleepwalking episodes.

Amethyst for a peaceful night free of insomnia, brings gentle dreams.

Citrine to understand dreams, experience shared dreams or to assist with dream journaling or dream study group sessions.

Lepidolite relieves confusion and disturbing thoughts which can block peaceful dreams.

Agate for varied and interesting dream journeys, aids in experiencing astral projection and shared dreams.

If sleep continues to be elusive, an effective technique to include with herbal brews, dream pillows and crystals involves numerology. After preparing for bedtime, with closed eyes visualize the number 100. Slowly count backward, seeing 99, 98, etc. Drift into the sleep state as the numbers melt away.

Good night and sweet dreams!

—DIKKI-JO MULLEN

35

A Musical Instrument

I

What was he doing, the great god Pan,
  Down in the reeds by the river?
Spreading ruin and scattering ban,
Splashing and paddling with hoofs of a goat,
And breaking the golden lilies afloat
  With the dragon-fly on the river.

II.

He tore out a reed, the great god Pan,
  From the deep cool bed of the river:
The limpid water turbidly ran,
And the broken lilies a-dying lay,
And the dragon-fly had fled away,
  Ere he brought it out of the river.

III.

High on the shore sate the great god Pan,
  While turbidly flowed the river;
And hacked and hewed as a great god can,
With his hard bleak steel at the patient reed,
Till there was not a sign of a leaf indeed
  To prove it fresh from the river.

36

IV.

He cut it short, did the great god Pan,
    (How tall it stood in the river!)
Then drew the pith, like the heart of a man,
Steadily from the outside ring,
And notched the poor dry empty thing
    In holes, as he sate by the river.

V.

This is the way,' laughed the great god Pan,
    (Laughed while he sat by the river,)
The only way, since gods began
To make sweet music, they could succeed.'
Then, dropping his mouth to a hole in the reed,
    He blew in power by the river.

VI.

Sweet, sweet, sweet, O Pan!
    Piercing sweet by the river!
Blinding sweet, O great god Pan!
The sun on the hill forgot to die,
And the lilies revived, and the dragon-fly
    Came back to dream on the river.

VII.

Yet half a beast is the great god Pan,
    To laugh as he sits by the river,
Making a poet out of a man:
The true gods sigh for the cost and pain,—
For the reed which grows nevermore again
    As a reed with the reeds in the river.

—ELIZABETH BROWNING

37

Cats are also of their kind, kind or unkind uncanny Witches or Witches Darlings oft times Impes. Best of all for Luck is a Black cat in a house. Therein bideth nere a Mouse — Therefore men say

Kiss a black Cat
It will make you fat
Kiss a white one
It will make you lone
Kiss a black pied wi' white
A sad day and a merry Night.
If you meet a black Cat
in the Night and can see nouct
but her two eyes shing like coles
then say as she stares at you
Stir about still
Wish me no ill.
Though it be dark
Thine eyes I mark.
Then seek in that Place the
next day and you will find two
Sixpences or two pieces of gold
for all I care, unless thou givst
me one for then I hope it will
be gold. — For as the saying is If
thou beest rich and givest nouct
thou'rt a poor Bitch

Excerpt from

The Witchcraft of Dame Darrel of York

38

Cats are also of their Kind, kind or unkind, uncanny Witches or Witches Darlings oft times Impes. Best of all for Luck is a Black cat in a house. Therein bideth nere a Mouse.—Therefore men say

> Kiss a black Cat
> It will make you fat
> Kiss a white one
> It will make you lone
> Kiss a black pied wi' white
> A sad day and a merry Night
> If you meet a black Cate in the Night and can see nout but her
> two eyes shining like coles, then say as she stares at you
> Stir about still,
> Wish me no ill.
> Though it be dark,
> Thine eyes I mark.

Then seek in that Place the next day and you will find two Sixpences or two pieces of gold, for all I care, *unless thou givst me one for then I hope it will be gold.*—For as the saying is If thou beest rich and givest nout thou'rt a poor Bitch.

Gambling with the Moon: Divination and Freedom

An Excerpt From Rachel Pollack's
A Walk through the Forest of Souls

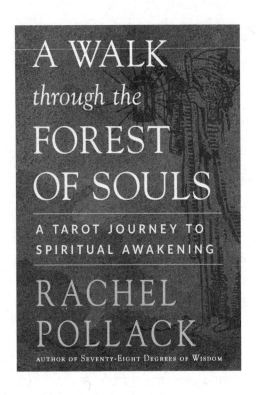

EGYPTIAN TALES often come in many variant forms, that is, different versions of the same basic story (like the Tarot itself, with all the different decks). For example, in the myth that follows, Thoth aids in the birth of Seth and Horus. But Horus is also the name of Seth's nephew, and in another story Seth somehow "impregnates" his nephew so that a golden disk grows on the young Horus's head, and eventually Horus "gives birth"—to none other than Thoth himself.

The following myth also comes in variant forms. In this version, Thoth gambles with the Moon. In other versions, Thoth himself is the Moon God and gambles with the other Gods

40

as a group. I've used the version below partly because it's the first one I read, and partly just because I like it and find it useful. This, too, is like Tarot. Many Tarotists who become collectors, and may own hundreds of decks, still read or do other work (meditation, for instance) with the first deck they saw, the deck that made them fall in love with Tarot.

Here, then, is Thoth and the Moon, with some details of my own invention.

Nut (rhymes with root), Goddess of the Night Sky, was married to Ra, the all-powerful God of the Sun. Like many wives, she strayed, and took up with Geb, the God of the Earth. Readers alert to esoteric symbolism will recognize this situation as the universal tale of spirit "descending" into matter, in other words, taking on a physical form. Many people see this theme in the Tarot card of The Fool, who steps off a cliff and will fall to Earth.

The Sun God represents pure light, which may be a metaphor for divine spirit, or may in fact be the very essence of spirit itself, the true nature of reality (we will return to this concept in later chapters). For creation to take place spirit must enter matter (we will see, in chapter thirteen, that we might describe matter, physical bodies, as light slowed down). The dark sky, married to light, must become the lover of Earth, and become pregnant. For this is how new things emerge, a new generation of Gods, or new ideas and discoveries, when we break the rules and allow ourselves to become pregnant.

When Ra discovers his wife pregnant from an affair, he issues a command. Nut will not bear her children on any day of any month of the year. Obviously, this means she must stay pregnant forever. We are dealing with the calendar and the zodiac here. The Egyptians imagined that before the birth of the new generation of Gods, those who would deal directly with human culture, the year consisted of twelve months of exactly thirty days each. Perfect regularity, the same clockwork existence over and over. This is the world of the sky, and not of Earth, where life is dynamic and ever-changing.

Clearly in a dilemma, Nut does the only sensible thing and turns to the expert of experts, Thoth. Now, we might expect that Thoth will persuade Ra, or find some ingenious solution (for those of you who remember Uncle Scrooge comic books, Thoth reminds me of the great inventor Gyro Gearloose). Instead, Thoth gambles. If you want to step outside a closed system, you cannot do so through plans within that system, you have to break it open. Gambling does this because it removes control. Thoth gambles with the Moon, who after all determines the months with its cycle of twenty-nine and a half days.

Again, I should comment that in most versions Thoth is himself the Moon God, and gambles with a group of the other Gods—I have stayed with the version as I first learned it.

As good a gambler as everything else, Thoth wins one seventy-second of each day to produce five extra days that stand independently and are not in any month of the year (360 divided by 72 equals 5). Nut gives birth to a baby each day: Seth, Osiris, Isis, Nephthys,

41

The High Priestss and Wheel of Fortune from the Rider tarot

and Horus. Isis appears in many Tarot decks as The High Priestess card, while Seth sometimes shows up in his Greek form of Typhon, as the serpent of destruction on The Wheel of Fortune card.

The five days at the end of the year, not in any month, became a time of celebration in Egypt, when the rigid rules of society relaxed, and perhaps people experimented with their lives and identities.

Let's stop for a moment and look at that number seventy-two. It appears later in the mythology as well, when Seth has decided to destroy Osiris. To help him, he brings together a group of seventy-two henchmen.

If we happen to know that the Kabbalists claimed there were seventy-two names for God, or that a famous name contains seventy-two letters, or even that the first translation of the Hebrew Bible into Greek was called the Septuagint because a commission of seventy-two scholars did the work, we will understand that seventy-two does not appear in the story as a random number. Nor does it appear only to produce five days out of three hundred sixty, for the relationship between seventy-two and three hundred sixty also is not a chance occurrence.

The zodiac consists of twelve star clusters, or constellations, that lie more or less in a flat plane (called the "ecliptic") created by the apparent paths of all the

42

principal planets. (One reason Pluto was "demoted" from planetary status was because its orbit does not lie along the ecliptic.) Because humans live such a short time the stars appear stationary in their seasonal positions year after year. In fact, due to a wobble in the Earth's orbit caused by the gravitational pull of the sun and moon, the constellations actually shift, very very slowly. Over the course of two thousand one hundred sixty years the constellations—the signs of the zodiac—shift an entire month in relation to the Earth. In other words, astrological calendars will say that the sun enters Aries on the spring equinox, but this is really an agreed-upon fiction. The sun has not actually entered Aries on the equinox for about four thousand years. Those who follow astrology should be aware that modern astrology is not in fact related to the actual positions of stars and planets. Some already know this, and there is a branch, called sidereal, that is based on the current sky. But if you are an Aries panicking you've secretly been a Pisces all along, don't panic! Regardless of these astronomical facts, your astrological sign remains intact and valid.

About two thousand years ago, around the time of Jesus, the sun began to enter Pisces, the sign of the fish, at the beginning of spring. This is one reason why Christ often is compared to a fish, and why bishops wear fish- shaped hats, called mitres. Since that time, the signs have shifted again, so that the sun enters Aquarius around the time of the equinox,

If you want to step outside a closed system, you cannot do so through plans within that system, you have to break it open. Gambling does this because it removes control. Thoth gambles with the Moon, who after all determines the months with its cycle of twenty-nine and a half days.

43

Can we learn to read Tarot like Thoth, that is, to gamble with our supposed fate and open it up to new possibilities?

and we get the expressions New Age, and Age of Aquarius.

My astrologer friends have pointed out to me that Western astrology actually follows the *signs*, not the constellations. That is, the sun is said to enter Aries in Spring because the sign of Aries bears qualities of Spring. Astrology, therefore, is more a *divinatory* system than an astronomical one.

What does all this have to do with Thoth and the number seventy-two? The amount of time for the full zodiac to turn around the Earth, the Great Year as Plato called it, is twenty-five thousand, nine hundred and twenty years (12 times 2160). The zodiac is a circle, and long ago, astrologers organized circles into three hundred sixty degrees (based upon the constellations, with an arbitrary designation of thirty degrees for each of the twelve signs). One degree of the Great Year, one three hundred sixtieth of twenty-five thousand, nine hundred and twenty, is seventy-two.

When Thoth gambles with the Moon—or the other Gods—to win one seventy-second of the year, he is opening up one degree of a fixed circle. Fate, closed destiny, opens, and new possibilities emerge into existence to change the course of humanity.

Seth uses seventy-two in exactly the opposite way—except negatively. Here is what he does to destroy Osiris: he measures him. While Osiris sleeps, Seth and his gang of seventy-two carefully measure every turn of the God's body. Then they construct a magnificent jeweled box that will exactly fit and enclose him. At a party they pretend to discover the box and Seth says, "Hey, I know. Let's play a game. Whoever can fit inside this box gets to keep it." With fake enthusiasm, the seventy-two all lie down, and like Cinderella's sisters none of them fit.

Finally, Osiris tries it, and of course it fits him so tightly he cannot get up. Seth and his henchmen slam on the top, nail it down, seal it with lead and float it off down the Nile. Osiris has suffocated to death (don't worry, his wife Isis retrieves him and with the aid of—who else, Thoth—brings him back to life).

When the seventy-two measure Osiris, they limit him to one degree of

44

the infinite circle of his possibilities. Such measurement suffocates, becomes a coffin. It is the same for us. Virtually from the moment of our birth, society measures us. Doctors measure our physical (and more and more our psychological) abilities, schools measure our intelligence and "aptitude" for future careers, bosses measure our worth, family and friends all measure our character. We measure and weigh our bodies to judge our attractiveness. Potential partners place us on a scale of one to ten. Polls measure our beliefs and convictions, corporations measure our tastes. With every measurement, the box becomes tighter, and more elaborate. Just like Osiris, we suffocate in a box that limits us to one degree of who we can become.

Why should a Tarot reading play this game? Any reading that defines you, that says you are such and such a person, or that describes your destiny in fixed terms, becomes part of Seth's gang of suffocators. Can we learn to read Tarot like Thoth, that is, to gamble with our supposed fate and open it up to new possibilities? Like the new Gods, born outside any day of the year, can we use divination to bring new things into our reality?

What game did Thoth play to create extra days? Some ancient versions of the old myth say dice, but ever since 1781 and *Le Monde Primitif*, we have known better. Thoth did not invent Tarot to describe a fixed universe. He invented it so he could go to the Moon and say "Want to play some cards?" The God of magic invented Tarot to liberate us from measurements.

—RACHEL POLLACK

A Walk through the Forest of Souls is available at redwheelweiser.com

Rachel Pollack (1945-2023) was the leading light and foremost influence on modern Tarot. Her bestselling book, Seventy-Eight Degrees of Wisdom, first published in 1980 and never out of print, is widely described as the "Bible of Tarot." She was also a great influence upon the science fiction, fantasy, and comics communities, as well as being a trailblazer within the transgender community. A master of many genres, Pollack is renowned for her run of issues #64-87 of Doom Patrol (Vertigo Comics), where she created the first transgender superhero. A prolific author of both fiction and non-fiction, her other books include A Walk Through the Forest of Souls, Unquenchable Fire, Godmother Night, *and The Fissure King. She was the creator of* The Shining Tribe Tarot *and wrote the books for numerous other decks, including* The Vertigo Tarot *and* Salvador Dali's Tarot. *Pollack taught at the famed Omega Institute for over thirty years.*

45

MOON GARDENING

BY PHASE

Sow, transplant, bud and graft   *Plow, cultivate, weed and reap*

NEW	First Quarter	FULL	Last Quarter	NEW
Plant above-ground crops with outside seeds, flowering annuals.	Plant above-ground crops with inside seeds.	Plant root crops, bulbs, biennials, perennials.		Do not plant.

BY PLACE IN THE ZODIAC

In general—plant and transplant crops that bear above ground when the Moon is in a watery sign: Cancer, Scorpio or Pisces. Plant and transplant root crops when the Moon is in Taurus or Capricorn; the other earthy sign, Virgo, encourages rot. The airy signs, Gemini, Libra and Aquarius, are good for some crops and not for others. The fiery signs, Aries, Leo and Sagittarius, are barren signs for most crops and best used for weeding, pest control and cultivating the soil.

Aries—*barren, hot and dry.* Favorable for planting and transplanting beets, onions and garlic, but unfavorable for all other crops. Good for weeding and pest control, for canning and preserving, and for all activities involving fire.

♉

Taurus—*fruitful, cold and dry.* Fertile, best for planting root crops and also very favorable for all transplanting as it encourages root growth. Good for planting crops that bear above ground and for canning and preserving. Prune in this sign to encourage root growth.

♊

Gemini—*barren, hot and moist.* The best sign for planting beans, which will bear more heavily. Unfavorable for other crops. Good for harvesting and for gathering herbs.

♋

Cancer—*fruitful, cold and moist.* Best for planting crops that bear above ground and very favorable for root crops. Dig garden beds when the Moon is in this sign, and everything planted in them will flourish. Prune in this sign to encourage growth.

♌

Leo—*barren, hot and dry.* Nothing should be planted or transplanted while the Moon is in the Lion. Favorable for weeding and pest control, for tilling and cultivating the soil, and for canning and preserving.

♍

Virgo—*barren, cold and dry.* Good for planting grasses and grains, but unfavorable for other crops. Unfavorable for canning and preserving, but favorable for

46

weeding, pest control, tilling and cultivating. Make compost when the Moon is in the Virgin and it will ripen faster.

♎

Libra—*fruitful, hot and moist.* The best sign to plant flowers and vines and somewhat favorable for crops that bear above the ground. Prune in this sign to encourage flowering.

♏

Scorpio—*fruitful, cold and moist.* Very favorable to plant and transplant crops that bear above ground, and favorable for planting and transplanting root crops. Set out fruit trees when the Moon is in this sign and prune to encourage growth.

♐

Sagittarius—*barren, hot and dry.* Favorable for planting onions, garlic and cucumbers, but unfavorable for all other crops, and especially unfavorable for transplanting. Favorable for canning and preserving, for tilling and cultivating the soil, and for pruning to discourage growth.

♑

Capricorn—*fruitful, cold and dry.* Very favorable for planting and transplanting root crops, favorable for flowers, vines, and all crops that bear above ground. Plant trees, bushes and vines in this sign. Prune trees and vines to strengthen the branches.

♒

Aquarius—*barren, hot and moist.* Favorable for weeding and pest control, tilling and cultivating the soil, harvesting crops, and gathering herbs. Somewhat favorable for planting crops that bear above ground, but only in dry weather or the seeds will tend to rot.

♓

Pisces—*fruitful, cold and moist.* Very favorable for planting and transplanting crops that bear above ground and favorable for flowers and all root crops except potatoes. Prune when the Moon is in the Fishes to encourage growth. Plant trees, bushes and vines in this sign.

Consult our Moon Calendar pages for phase and place in the zodiac circle. The Moon remains in a sign for about two and a half days. Match your gardening activity to the day that follows the Moon's entry into that zodiacal sign. For best results, choose days when the phase and sign are both favorable. For example, plant seeds when the Moon is waxing in a suitable fruitful sign, and uproot stubborn weeds when the Moon is in the fourth quarter in a barren sign.

47

The MOON *Calendar*

is divided into zodiac signs rather
than the more familiar Gregorian calendar.

2024

2025

Bear in mind that new projects
should be initiated when the Moon
is waxing (from dark to full). When
the Moon is on the wane (from full
to dark), it is a time for storing
energy and the wise person waits.

Please note that Moons are listed by day of entry into each sign. Quarters
are marked, but as rising and setting times vary from one region to another,
it is advisable to check your local newspaper, library or planetarium.
The Moon's Place is computed for Eastern Time.

48

aries

March 20 – April 19, 2024

Cardinal Sign of Fire △ Ruled by Mars ♂

S	M	T	W	T	F	S
Kukulcan—*Sky, storms, war, creation* Transcending the barriers of ethnicity and language, Kukulcan is the Mesoamerican war serpent God. His ↓	Mar **19** Vernal Equinox	**20** *Light a candle* Leo	**21**	**22** *Buy seeds* Virgo	**23**	
24 Partial Lunar Eclipse ⇨	**25** Seed Moon Libra	**26** WANING	**27** Scorpio	**28** *Activate wards*	**29**	**30** *Dance* Sagittarius
31 *Tell a story*	April **1** Capricorn	**2** All Fools' Day ⇦	**3** *Sing* Aquarius	**4**	**5** *Note your dreams* Pisces	**6**
7 Total Solar Eclipse ⇨ Aries	**8**	**9** WAXING Taurus	**10**	**11** *Be patient* Gemini	**12**	**13** *Be kind* Cancer
14	**15**	**16** *Roar!* Leo	**17**	**18** Virgo	**19** *Prepare your garden*	

worship could be found from central Mexico to Nicaragua. Legend has it that Kukulcan was snake born, given into the care of his sister. She soon realized that he was of divine lineage and that he was the plumed serpent. As he grew, she took him to a cave to keep him safe. Growing too large for the cave, he flew off to the sea, causing an earthquake. He lets all know that he is alive by causing an earthquake every July. His worship was centered in the Yucatan among the Maya. At the Equinoxes, Kukulcan can be seen descending his stepped pyramid as the shadow cast by the staircase creates the body for the serpent head at the northern base.

The Geomantic Figures: Conjunctio

GEOMANCY IS AN ANCIENT SYSTEM of divination that uses sixteen symbols, the geomantic figures. Easy to learn and use, it was one of the most popular divination methods in the Middle Ages and Renaissance. It remained in use among rural cunning folk for many centuries thereafter, and is now undergoing a renaissance of its own as diviners discover its possibilities.

The geomantic figures are made up of single and double dots. Each figure has a name and a divinatory meaning, and the figures are also assigned to the four elements, the twelve signs of the Zodiac, the seven planets and the nodes of the Moon. The dots that make up the figures signify their inner meanings: the four lines of dots represent Fire, Air, Water and Earth, and show that the Elements are present in either active (one dot) or latent (two dots) form.

The sixth of the geomantic figures is Conjunctio, which means Conjunction. Conjunctio belongs to the element of Earth, the Zodiacal sign Virgo, and the planet Mercury (or in some accounts, the dwarf planet Ceres.) The pattern of dots that forms this figure resembles a crossroads, where travelers from many different places can meet and exchange news.

Read as symbols of the Elements, the dots that form Conjunctio reveal much about the nature of this figure. In this figure the middle Elements Air and Water are active, and Fire and Earth, which form the extremes of the elemental spectrum, are latent. As water evaporates into mist and vapor and then condenses back into liquid to fall as rain, the Elements of Air and Water mingle and exchange qualities.

In divination Conjunctio stands for interaction, exchange and contact with others. It is neither fortunate nor unfortunate, and commonly means that good fortune and misfortune will be mixed together. It is favorable for questions involving fertility, however, and for the recovery of things that have been lost or stolen.

–JOHN MICHAEL GREER

50

taurus

April 20 – May 20, 2024

Fixed Sign of Earth ▽ Ruled by Venus ♀

S	M	T	W	T	F	S

Ba'al Hadad—*Storms, thunder, rain* With a lightning bolt in one hand and a mace in the other, Ba'al Hadad (Ba'al meaning "lord") is a formidable deity of storms and thunder. As the master of rain, he was also associated with the fertility of fields and humans alike. Of the many epithets that Hadad bore, Rider of the Clouds is most the apt. His chief consort was the Goddess Atargatis who also was associated with the fertility of the fields. His absence was said to bring drought that in turn brought death. His mythology often speaks of his ↓ — April **20**

21 Libra	**22** *Carry moonstone*	**23** (Hare Moon) Scorpio	**24** WANING	**25**	**26** *Wear lavender* Sagittarius	**27**
28 *Clean house* Capricorn	**29**	**30** *Walpurgis Night* Aquarius	May **1**	**2** Beltane ⇦ *Gather dew*	**3** Pisces	**4**
5 Aries	**6** *Scry at midnight*	**7** Taurus	**8** WAXING White Lotus Day	**9** Gemini	**10** *Talk to the bees*	**11** Cancer
12	**13** Leo	**14** *Brew hot tea*	**15**	**16** Virgo	**17**	**18** *Hold tight to memories* Libra
19	**20**	strength which was said to be stronger than all the deities in his pantheon. His stormy nature and incredible strength allowed him to become the chief of Gods. When the chief God El sought to elevate his own son Yam, Hadad opposed the move and went to war with Yam. By means of this battle as well as others, Hadad eventually supplanted El.				

51

Tibetan Singing Bowls

SINGING BOWLS are a type of bell traditionally used in Tibetan Buddhist meditation practices. Also known as Himalayan bowls or Tibetan bowls, these metal bowls are used for a variety of purposes including chanting, singing and instrumental music. The bowls are struck or played with a mallet to produce a rich, soothing sound believed to have therapeutic and calming effects on the mind and body.

The history of singing bowls in Tibet can be traced back to ancient times. Used in spiritual ceremonies and rituals, singing bowls are powerful tools for cultivating mindfulness and inner peace. In Tibetan culture singing bowls are considered to be sacred objects and are typically treated with great reverence. They are often passed down from generation to generation and some very old bowls are quite valuable.

To play a singing bowl, strike the rim of the bowl with a mallet or striker for a bell-like tone or rub the rim with a circular motion to produce a rich, harmonious sound that is both soothing and uplifting. Some practitioners believe that the vibrations produced by the bowl can help to clear negative energy and promote healing and balance in the body.

Singing bowls come in a variety of sizes and shapes. Some bowls are small and portable while others are large and require a stand to be played. The bowls are typically made from a blend of metals, including copper, tin, iron and other trace elements. The specific combination of metals used in the creation of a singing bowl affects its sound and spiritual properties. The price of a singing bowl can vary widely depending on the size, quality and materials used in its construction. Some bowls are hand-crafted by skilled artisans, while others are mass-produced. It is important to do research and purchase from a reputable dealer to ensure that you are getting a high quality bowl that is made with care and attention to detail.

There are various ways to incorporate singing bowls into daily life and spiritual practices. You can use them as part of a daily meditation routine or incorporate them into yoga or other physical practices to achieve relaxation and clarity. Singing bowls can also be used in group settings such as in group meditation or yoga classes, where the sound of the bowls helps to create a sense of unity and connection among participants. They are also used in music therapy and as a form of stress relief. Many people find the sound of the bowls to be deeply relaxing and find that listening to them helps to calm the mind and promote feelings of wellbeing.

However you choose to use singing bowls, they can be a powerful tool for cultivating mindfulness and inner peace whether you are an experienced practitioner or are just beginning to explore the world of sacred sound.

gemini
May 21 – June 20, 2024
Mutable Sign of Air △ Ruled by Mercury ☿

S	M	T	W	T	F	S
		May **21** Scorpio	**22** Vesak Day	**23** (Dyad Moon) Sagittarius	**24** WANING	**25** Capricorn
26	**27**	**28** *Accept criticism* Aquarius	**29** Oak Apple Day Pisces	**30** (waning gibbous moon)	**31**	June **1** Aries
2 *Negate evil*	**3** Taurus	**4**	**5** Night of the Watchers Gemini	**6** (new moon)	**7** WAXING Cancer	**8** *Speak to your father*
9 Leo	**10**	**11** *Take precautions*	**12** Virgo	**13** *Feed the birds*	**14** (first quarter moon)	**15** Libra
16	**17** *Light incense* Scorpio	**18**	**19** *Greet the sun* Sagittarius	**20** Summer Solstice	**Manannán mac Lir—** *Sea, truth, immortality* Lending his name to the Isle of Man, Manannán mac Lir is God of the Sea. Like many deities of the Celtic Irish,	

he was one of the Tuatha de Danann. Manannán is found in the lore of Gaelic speakers. In Ireland and the Isle of Man it is folk custom to make offerings at the Summer Solstice to ward off invaders coming by sea. As a warrior, Manannán was said to have armor that was impenetrable and an enchanted sword that no enemy could survive. Manannán had a strong connection with truth, evidenced by his sword (named the Answerer) held against the throat of any would allow only the truth to pass the lips of the subject. He also was the owner of a golden cup which would break if three untruths were spoken over it.

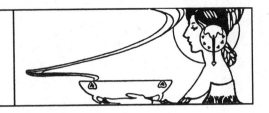

KITCHEN MAGIC

Poolish

THE MAGIC of cooking is timeless, and its oldest processes are some of the most magical. The process of turning barley to ale or wheat to bread is certainly causing dramatic change in accordance with will, but it is more, too. When a fermenting brew begins to fizz, when a seemingly inanimate blob of levain or sourdough dramatically rises and threatens to bubble over onto the countertop, there is ancient magic—it is like a quickening. Where there was potential, there is now life, and that life will be consumed to sustain more life. To touch that mystery in the modern kitchen, begin by mixing just a tiny pinch of yeast into equal amounts of water and flour. They should be equal by weight, or two parts flour to one part water by volume. Wait overnight and then—*abracadabra!*—the bubbling beast is ready to become a loaf! This is the process of making a *poolish*, a type preferment used to add complex flavor and extensibility to baguettes and other continental breads, but you can substitute a sourdough starter in the same amounts if you are lucky and committed enough to be keeping one.

Making a Poolish

¼ cup room-temperature water
½cup flour
tiniest pinch of yeast possible.
1 ½ cups cold water
4 ½ cups bread flour
2 teaspoons salt
½ teaspoon yeast

Thoroughly mix the first three ingredients, cover loosely and allow to sit at room temperature for 12 to 18 hours. Stir in remaining ingredients to make a sticky dough. Using a wet hand, grab a side of the dough, stretch it up and fold over to the other side. Turn the bowl 90 degrees and repeat, 5 or 6 then cover and allow to rest at room temperature. Repeat the folds every 20 minutes for an hour, then allow to rise. When the dough has doubled in size, punch all the air out of it and turn it out onto a floured countertop. With a floured hand, scoop your hands under the loaf, turning and tucking in the sides to create a round shape. Slide onto a floured cookie sheet. Allow to rise again. Heat oven to at least 425 degrees, placing a pan of water on the bottom rack to create steam. Cut several deep slashes across the top of the loaf and bake until tapping on the bottom produces a hollow sound.

—MAB BORDEN

54

cancer

June 21 – July 22, 2024
Cardinal Sign of Water ▽ Ruled by Moon ☽

CANCER

S	M	T	W	T	F	S
	Veles—*Earth, livestock, the Underworld* A primal deity—Veles can be encountered universally in the pantheons of the Slavs. Seemingly, his importance to the Slavs persisted beyond the Christianization of Europe. A shapeshifting deity, he assumes many forms throughout his mythology. When he appears in the form of a serpent or a dragon, he is the ruler ↓				June **21** Mead Moon	**22** WANING Capricorn
23 Gather St. John's Wort	**24** Midsummer Aquarius	**25**	**26** Dream of the Faeries Pisces	**27**	**28** Aries	**29**
30 Taurus	July **1** Jump for luck	**2** Gemini	**3** Cast an enchantment	**4**	**5** Cancer	**6** WAXING
7 Cleanse doorways Leo	**8**	**9** Virgo	**10** Pick flowers	**11**	**12** Libra	**13**
14 Scorpio	**15** Polish silver	**16**	**17** Sagittarius	**18** Invoke Mars	**19** Capricorn	**20** Greet the Moon
21 Aquarius	**22** WANING	of the Underworld who sits beneath the roots of the World Tree. In another manifestation, he is the ruler of the deep forests appearing as an elk-horned God. In this manifestation Veles is ruling over yet another liminal world. The myths of Veles often relate stories of his rivalry with the God of thunder and the sky, Perun. Their battles illuminate Nature's cycle of dry and wet seasons—the wetness is vanquished and killed only to resurrect to battle again.				

木
龍

YEAR OF THE WOOD DRAGON
February 10, 2024–January 28, 2025

THE DRAGON is the fifth of the twelve animal signs in the Chinese Zodiac. It is the only supernatural creature among the animals, each of which represents a year. Five elements (fire, water, metal, earth and wood) are also a part of this oldest of the world's zodiac/calendars. Chinese New Year commences with the second New Moon after the Winter Solstice. This places the lunar New Year in late January to mid-February, almost always at the New Moon in Aquarius.

Dragon years are thought to be most auspicious. Good luck, health and strength are on the rise. As an emblem of authority and power, Dragon is portrayed holding a magical pearl in his mouth. This precious jewel represents both the Moon and Sun as well as the spiritual essence of the universe. The species of Dragons are differentiated by the five elements. 2024 brings the Green Wood Dragon. The Wood element is the personification of growth and development. Its color, green, carries a positive association with the flowering of nature and new life. The wise will be cautious when considering gambles. The year's electrical atmosphere can generate folly. The mighty Dragon ushers in surprises which often will upset the status quo. Those born during a Dragon year are described as being flamboyant, intelligent and good leaders.

More information on the Wood Dragon can be found on our website at http://TheWitchesAlmanac.com/pages/almanac-extras

Years of the Dragon
1928, 1940, 1952, 1964, 1976, 1988, 2000, 2012, 2024

Illustration by Ogmios MacMerlin

56

leo

July 23 – August 22, 2024

Fixed Sign of Fire △ Ruled by Sun ☉

♌ LEO

S	M	T	W	T	F	S
		July **23** Ancient Egyptian New Year Pisces	**24**	**25** Recite an old prayer Aries	**26**	**27**
28 Taurus	**29** Harvest Corn	**30** Gemini	**31** Lughnassad Eve	Aug **1** Lammas Cancer	**2** Bake bread	**3** Leo
4	**5** WAXING	**6** Make libations Virgo	**7**	**8** Arrive safely Libra	**9**	**10**
11 Scorpio	**12**	**13** Diana's Day Sagittarius	**14**	**15** Capricorn	**16** Take heed	**17** Black Cat Appreciation Day
18 Brace yourself Aquarius	**19** Wort Moon	**20** WANING Pisces	**21** Enjoy sea waves	**22** Aries	**Ò rúnmìlà—*Truth, destiny, knowledge*** Bearing witness to all of creation, it is Òrúnmìlà the Òrìṣà (divinity) who can relate all that was, all that is and all that	

will be into eternity. He is among the primordial Òrìṣà who emanated from Olódùmarè (the high God) before any of physical creation came into being and as such bears the appellation of Irunmole. Among his many praise names are Ibikeji Olódùmarè (second only to Olódùmarè) and Elérìí ìpín (witness of destiny.) The secrets of the universe and the secrets of each individual are said to be encoded in the poetry that is called Ifá that is the provenance of the Babaláwo (father of secrets) and Ìyánífá (Mother of Ifá,) the priests of Òrúnmìlà. The sacred poetry holds the lore of each of the Òrìṣà and the proper way in which to live a successful life.

Thoreau's Journal (14 volumes!).
Oct. 5, 1851—MOONLIGHT AND FAIRIES

To appreciate the moonlight, you must stand in the shade and see where a few rods or a few feet distant it falls in between the trees. It is a "milder day," made for some inhabitants whom you do not see. The fairies are a quiet, gentle folk, invented plainly to inhabit the moonlight. I frequently see a light on the ground within thick and dark woods where all around is in shadow, and haste forward, expecting to find some decayed and phosphorescent stump, but find it to be some clear moonlight that falls in between some crevice in the leaves. As moonlight is to sunlight, so are the fairies to men.

—The Journal of Henry David Thoreau,
Vol. III September and October, 1851 (ÆT. 34),
Boston: Houghton Miffline Co., 1906, p. 47.

58

virgo

August 23 – September 22, 2024

Mutable Sign of Earth ♍ Ruled by Mercury ☿

S	M	T	W	T	F	S
Jupiter—*The sky, thunder and lightning, justice* The fearsome king of the Gods, Jupiter—who was also known as Jove—was chief among a large pantheon of Gods worshipped in the Roman Empire. He was often depicted holding the thunderbolt or seated with an eagle. The two symbols were combined and used as a martial emblem by the armies of Rome. Such was Jupiter's association with eagles that it was said that he could take the form ↓					Aug **23**	**24** Taurus
25	**26** Gemini	**27**	**28** *Perform a water blessing* Cancer	**29**	**30** *Know honor* Leo	**31**
Sept **1**	**2** Virgo	**3** WAXING	**4**	**5** *Make a brew* Libra	**6** Ganesh Chaturthi	**7** Scorpio
8	**9** *Uncover a lie* Sagittarius	**10**	**11**	**12** Capricorn	**13** *A harvest day*	**14** Aquarius
15 *Drink cool water*	**16** *Eat sparingly* Pisces	**17** Barley Moon	**18** Partial Lunar Eclipse ⇐	**19** WANING ⇐ Aries ⇐	**20** Taurus	**21**
22 Autumnal Equinox Gemini	of an eagle. Jupiter also had a strong association with justice. Oaths were sworn before him. In ancient times Jupiter was worshipped in a sanctuary on Mons Albanus. In legend, king Tullus Hostilius destroyed it, relocating all the residents of Alba to Rome. Because the Albans discontinued his worship, Jupiter caused a rain of rocks and a plague, which eventually took the life of Tullus. The Albans heeded the signs and again worshiped him.					

TAROT'S TEMPERANCE

TEMPERANCE REPRESENTS the third of the four Cardinal Virtues. The Catholic theologian Thomas Aquinas said a man possessed of Temperance fulfilled the condition of being "restrained within measure." In the Tarot, Temperance is today depicted as a woman pouring liquid from one container into another, maybe diluting wine with water. This was her standard iconographical form in Western art. Most likely she replaced the original figure of Ganymede, a young Trojan prince with whom Zeus fell in love and abducted to become his wine-pourer and cupbearer. Temperance was considered by moralizing scholastic theologians to be the Virtue that specifically took aim at the Deadly Sin of Wrath, although more modern interpreters would consider Gluttony, which includes Drunkenness, to be her chief foe. Giovanni Piscina, however, writing in 1565, states that Temperance takes this position in the trump sequence as she represents *all* the Virtues that do not fear Death, and therefore she is placed in triumph above him.

Excerpted from Dame Fortune's Wheel Tarot—A Pictorial Key *by Paul Huson, published by The Witches' Almanac.*

libra

September 23 – October 22, 2024
Cardinal Sign of Air ♎ Ruled by Venus ♀

LIBRA

S	M	T	W	T	F	S
	Sept **23**	**24** ◐ Cancer	**25**	**26**	**27** Dry herbs Leo	**28**
29 Virgo	**30** Turn around three times	Oct **1** Partial Solar Eclipse ⇨	**2** ● Libra	**3** WAXING	**4** Scorpio	**5** Bite your tongue
6 Balance your budget Sagittarius	**7**	**8**	**9** Capricorn	**10** ◐	**11** Appreciate art Aquarius	**12**
13 Pisces	**14** Beware of the evil eye	**15** Aries	**16**	**17** Blood Moon	**18** WANING Taurus	**19** Meditate
20 Gemini	**21**	**22** Cast a healing spell Cancer				

Krishna—*Music, compassion, love* One of the most-worshipped Gods of the Hindu pantheons, Krishna is the eighth avatar (incarnation) of the God Vishnu. His name is derived from Sanskrit meaning "dark blue." It is said that as a baby Krishna sucked poisoned milk from a demon who in an attempt to kill him disguised herself as a woman. Rather than killing him, the poison caused his skin to turn blue. In the corpus of Hindu literature, Krishna figures prominently, appearing as a child, a hero, a lover and even as the universal supreme God known as Svayam Bhagavan. In many early Hindu texts, Krishna is shown as an independent God rather than an avatar of Vishnu. It was said that in the body of Krishna existed the essence of man. In his many abilities and his many guises, Krishna is always the embodiment and essence of divine love—the Gods' love for mankind and the love of humans for the Gods. It's believed that when Krishna plays his flute, the sound is only heard by enlightened beings.

COUNTING CROWS

One for sorrow,

Two for joy,

Three for a girl,

Four for a boy,

Five for silver,

Six for gold,

Seven for a secret never to be told.

Eight for a wish,

Nine for a kiss,

Ten a surprise you should be careful not to miss,

Eleven for health,

Twelve for wealth,

Thirteen beware it's the devil himself.

scorpio

October 23 – November 21, 2024
Fixed Sign of Water ▽ *Ruled by Pluto* ♀

SCORPIVS

S	M	T	W	T	F	S
Cernunnos—***Otherworld, Wild Things*** Seated among the wild beasts of the forest, Cernunnos can be found in one form or another across the wide expanse of the Celtic nations of yore. While his name varied, at the root is *karn*, which means antler or horn. ↓			Oct **23**	**24** Leo	**25**	**26** Virgo
27	**28** *Black mirror gazing*	**29** Libra	**30** *Use the cards*	**31** Samhain Eve	Nov **1** Scorpio	**2** WAXING Hallowmas ⇐
3 Sagittarius	**4** *Ouija speaks*	**5** Capricorn	**6**	**7** *Gift garlic*	**8** Aquarius	**9**
10 Pisces	**11**	**12** *Light a candle* Aries	**13**	**14** Taurus	**15** Snow Moon	**16** WANING Hecate Night Gemini
17	**18** Cancer	**19** *Eat chocolate*	**20** *Take cover* Leo	**21**		

His iconography consistently depicts him as a seated God displaying antlers on his head. In many depictions he holds in one hand a symbol of fertility or abundance such as a shaft of wheat, a bag of coins or a cornucopia. In the other hand he may be found holding a torque—a symbol of wealth as well as a symbol of the Gods. Often he is seen with a stag or a ram-horned serpent. On some of his iconography, he is surrounded by the animals of the forest. His images suggests that the Celts considered him a deity of the wilds and an otherworldly guardian of departed souls. To many modern Witches he is the Horned God, consort of the Great Goddess.

Statue of a Satyr
Pompeii, Italy

sagittarius

November 22 – December 21, 2024

Mutable Sign of Fire △ Ruled by Jupiter ♃

S	M	T	W	T	F	S
Mithra—**Covenant, judgement, light, Sun** Crossing the Bridge of Separation, every soul must meet with three beings who will sit in judgement of their life. Mithra was one among these three who would appraise the thoughts, words and deeds of the lifetime of the soul before them. The God of the Sun whose blinding light beholds all that is, he is to this day invoked in the taking of oaths. According to some myths Mithras was born beside a sacred stream under ↓					Nov **22** ◐	**23** Virgo
24 Call a friend	**25** Watch Birds Libra	**26**	**27** Write a poem	**28** Scorpio	**29**	**30** Create a talisman Sagittarius
Dec **1** ●	**2** WAXING	**3** Collect acorns Capricorn	**4**	**5** Enjoy freedom Aquarius	**6**	**7** Take heed tonight Pisces
8 ◐	**9** Recognize your fears Aries	**10**	**11** Taurus	**12**	**13** Smile all day Gemini	**14**
15 Oak Moon	**16** WANING Fairy Queen Eve Cancer	**17** Saturnalia	**18** Tell jokes Leo	**19**	**20** Drink herbal tea Virgo	**21** Winter Solstice

a sacred tree bearing a torch and a knife. There is a strong connection between the act of creation and Mithra. In pre-Zoroaster myth it was Mithra who slew the Cosmic Bull from whose blood all of creation leapt. In later myths, he is not the creator but rather the ruler of the Earth. The evolution of Mithra perhaps started in India as Mitra, the Vedic God of integrity associated with the Sun. Arriving in Persia, he became Mithra the God of Light and truth and when he finally arrived in Rome, he became Mithras, a favorite of the Roman legions.

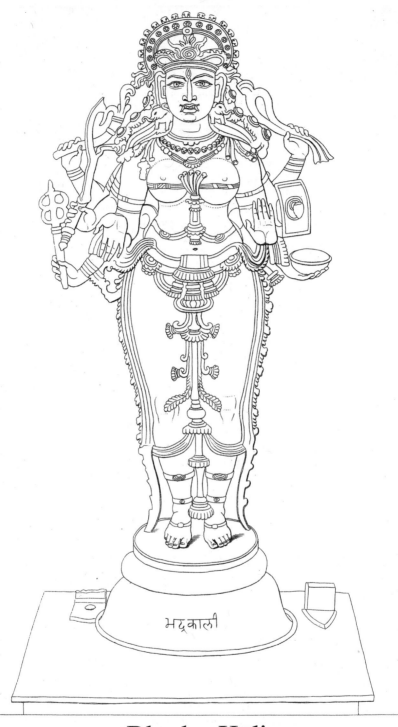

भद्रकाली

Bhadra Kāli
From a Bronze Statue

66

capricorn

December 22 2024 – January 19, 2025

Cardinal Sign of Earth ▽ Ruled by Saturn ♄

S	M	T	W	T	F	S
Osiris—*Vegetation, Fertility, the dead* The eldest son of Geb and Nut, Osiris was one of the most prominent among the pantheon of Gods who were worshipped in ancient Egypt. He is best known as the God who was once killed by his brother Set and resurrected by his sister-wife Isis. The myth relates that upon killing Osiris, Set cut up his remains and tossed them into the Nile River. Upon learning the fate of her husband-brother, Isis set out to collect ↓						Dec **21** *Sit in silence*
22	**23** Libra	**24** *Play a game*	**25** Scorpio	**26**	**27** *Wear a hat* Sagittarius	**28**
29 *Achieve success!*	**30** Capricorn	**31** WAXING	Jan **1** *Gather facts* Aquarius	**2**	**3** Pisces	**4** *Fill your cauldron*
5 Aries	**6**	**7**	**8** *Eat preserves* Taurus	**9** Feast of Janus	**10** *Do a reading* Gemini	**11**
12 *Make a wish* Cancer	**13** Wolf Moon	**14** WANING Leo	**15**	**16** *Plan a dinner party* Virgo	**17**	**18**
19 Libra	the scattered bits of body, finding all except the phallus that a fish had eaten. Fashioning a phallus of gold, she reunited all pieces and brought Osiris back to life. Osiris was the God of death and resurrection from that time. Known as the Lord of Silence, Osiris sits in judgement of all who would enter the world of the dead. Wearing a crown that is similar to that of the crown of Upper Egypt, he was long associated with the royalty of Egypt and their eternal existence after death. Often depicted with green skin, he also ruled over the farming cycle.					

⋛ Alder ⋚

Fearn

THE FIRST THREE TREES of the alphabet flourish on heights and mountain slopes. By contrast, the alder is usually found thriving in thickets beside lakes, streams and rivers. It so favors marshy conditions that the tree seldom grows on drier land. Its black bark scored with cracks and broad oval leaves quickly identify the alder. As the timber dries after felling, its color changes from yellow to orange to red. When dried, the wood is water resistant and does not split when nailed. For centuries alder has provided pilings to serve as building foundations throughout European lowlands. Charcoal derived from alder wood is superior to all others.

The alder is associated with Bran, a Celtic hero/ god. One tale about him is found in the medieval Welsh collection of legends known as *The Mabinogion*. Another story, *The Voyage of Bran to the World Below*, occurs in Irish literature recorded in the 8th century. The sea-god Llyr (Welsh) and Lir (Irish) plays a role in both tales as do black birds: the starling, crow and raven. The Irish epic describes Bran waking from a dream to find himself in the presence of a goddess and holding in his hand a silver branch. The branch magically springs from his hand to hers once he agrees to set sail for the abode of the goddess.

It is rare to find alder mentioned in European folklore. Old herbals, however, submit many practical uses for alder leaves.

68

aquarius

January 20 – February 18, 2025

Fixed Sign of Air ♎ *Ruled by Uranus* ♅

S	M	T	W	T	F	S
	Jan **20**	**21** ◑ Scorpio	**22**	**23** Visit friends	**24** Sagittarius	**25**
26 Capricorn	**27** Call the spirits	**28** Chinese New Year ⇨	**29** ● Aquarius	**30** WAXING	**31** Pisces	Feb **1** Oimelc Eve
2 Candlemas Aries	**3** Clean your home	**4** Taurus	**5** ◑	**6** Read a book Gemini	**7** Roll dice	**8** Cancer
9	**10** Pet your familiar Leo	**11** Cast a circle	**12** (Storm Moon)	**13** WANING Virgo	**14**	**15** Lupercalia Libra
16 Feel the Sun	**17**	**18** Drain the cup Scorpio				

Thor—*Thunder, lightning, fertility* Fiercest among the Norse pantheon, Thor is the son of the All-Father Odin. He is known as the owner of thunder and lightning, which is generated by his hammer named Mjölnir. Thor also has a strong association with masculinity and virility, with an unrelenting sexual appetite. Because these qualities are so prominent, as well as his storms, he is also considered to be a God of fertility. Thor is the epitome of the God-hero, always brave and righteous. With his hammer in hand and girded with Megingjörd (belt of power) and gloved with Járngreipr (iron grippers,) he faced all challenges with ferocity and determination. While Thor's father Odin was the highest of the Aesir Gods, his mother was the giantess Jord. Thor's mythology spread far and wide, figuring prominently where Norse and Germanic peoples settled. In fact, to the present day there are folk customs that are strongly associated with Thor in modern German populations.

69

The Ass and His Shadow

A TRAVELER HAD HIRED an Ass to carry him to a distant part of the country. The owner of the Ass went with the Traveler, walking beside him to drive the Ass and point out the way.

The road led across a treeless plain where the Sun beat down fiercely. So intense did the heat become, that the Traveler at last decided to stop for a rest, and as there was no other shade to be found, the Traveler sat down in the shadow of the Ass.

Now the heat had affected the Driver as much as it had the Traveler, and even more, for he had been walking. Wishing also to rest in the shade cast by the Ass, he began to quarrel with the Traveler, saying he had hired the Ass and not the shadow it cast.

The two soon came to blows, and while they were fighting, the Ass took to its heels.

In quarreling about the shadow we often lose the substance.

pisces
February 19 – March 20, 2025
Mutable Sign of Water ▽ Ruled by Neptune ♆

S	M	T	W	T	F	S
Raijin—*Thunder, lightning, storms* Beating his drums while standing on a cloud and red with anger, Raijin is the Shinto God of storms. Fiercest among the Gods, he is often in the company of Fujin, the God of the Winds. Raijin is depicted holding ↓			Feb **19**	**20** ◑ Sagittarius	**21**	**22**
23 Capricorn	**24**	**25** *Play games* Aquarius	**26** *Drink chamomile before bed*	**27** ● Pisces	**28** WAXING	Mar **1** Matronalia Aries
2	**3** *Bake cookies* Taurus	**4**	**5** *Call a friend* Gemini	**6** ◐	**7** *Skip a meal* Cancer	**8**
9 *Watch the sunrise* Leo	**10**	**11**	**12** *Bury chains* Virgo	**13** Total Lunar Eclipse ⇨	**14** Chaste Moon	**15** WANING Libra
16	**17** Scorpio	**18** *Avoid conflict today*	**19** Minerva's Day	**20** Vernal Equinox Sagittarius		

the hammers with which he beats out his thunderous tunes during storms. He is a muscular, bare-chested deity, his unruly hair revealing his uncontrollable nature. While seemingly malevolent in appearance, he is often depicted with a halo to indicate his spiritual place in the pantheon. He brings the rains necessary for farming. He is also the defender of temples. He embodies destruction as well as life. Shinto priests teach that Raijin is the trickster *kami* (spirit.) Raijin is said to ignore the prayers and pleadings of priests and emperor. Raijin was born from the body of the rotting corpse of Izanami, the Mother Goddess of all the deities.

71

WE ARE STARDUST

EVERY ATOM in your body came from the belly of a star. The only exception is the primordial hydrogen inside of you which formed at the Big Bang. Otherwise, your atoms—six and a half octillion of them—came to you from long-dead supernovas. That's a 65 followed by 26 zeros!

Several billion years ago in the Milky Way galaxy the first generation of large stars reached the end of their lives and exploded. These Little Bangs spread their atoms out in expanding spheres at near light speed. Immense clouds of atoms drew towards each other, like attracting like, compressed and ignited in acts of creation to manifest new stars. The largest stars repeated this cycle of igniting, shining and exploding maybe three or four times. The Sun is at least a second generation star born of supernova dust. Some of that dust was not sent swirling into the Sun during creation but remained rotating around him. Everything in near space to Earth

72

came from this same ancient star-stuff and some of that became...just look in a mirror! Sun, Moon, Mother Earth and you are all physical siblings.

For about five billion years the Sun has forged helium from hydrogen. This transmutation releases the energy that sustains almost all of life on Earth. In about another five billion years the Sun will die but because of his smaller size he will not explode like his supernova ancestors. He will instead at first expand into a red giant and then shrink into a white dwarf, creating some oxygen and carbon late in life that he will retain well into retirement.

The oxygen and carbon on Earth today came from the same supernovas that spawned the Sun. These also transmuted helium from hydrogen, but having been so much larger these stellar furnaces continued to burn helium and forge carbon, nitrogen, and oxygen along with additional atoms that were heavier, larger and more complex than the Sun could ever create. Eventually they came to produce iron and exploded when iron production concluded. At that moment of explosion, the energy expended could cause a single star to shine brighter than a whole galaxy! Atoms beyond iron—trans-ferric atoms—were instantly forged and blasted through space.

Humans are born of supernovas. Your body is two-thirds oxygen. Add hydrogen, carbon, and nitrogen and you've accounted for 96% of yourself. Beyond those basic four, you possess about eighty other types of atoms, including even a tiny amount of gold!

As the stars are above, so we are below. As atoms are within, so atoms are without.

Someday an astronomer may identify the stellar remains of the supernovas that spawned the Sun, human atoms contemplating the ancient cradle. You are stardust. You are golden. You are several-billion-year-old carbon. You are the Universe, examining itself.

—STELLUX

73

A Famous Haunting and the Bell Witch Fall Festival of Adams, Tennessee

EACH YEAR on weekends from late September through mid-October those who enjoy paranormal studies and Witchery can attend a unique Fall festival. The Bell Witch Festival in Adams, Tennessee (population about 690) is North of Nashville on Hwy 41 near the Kentucky border. The popular event features art, music, history and folklore. The festival's star is Kate, the Bell Witch.

Dubbed, "the most documented supernatural event in American history" by the Tennessee Department of Tourist Development, the story of the Bell Witch has made the tiny hamlet of Adams famous. Many incidents of the haunting date from the early 1800s

to recent happenings. The Bell Witch Cave, located on the property once owned by the Bell family, is the scene of many paranormal phenomena. The cave has been placed on the National Register of Historic Places by the United States Department of the Interior. The Bell Witch Cave is over 400 feet long and houses a number of artifacts from the original home and farm which once stood on the property.

It all began in 1804 when a settler named John Bell purchased a farm on the Red River near what is now the town of Adams. He built a six-room home for his wife Lucy and their nine children. For about thirteen years the Bell family lived there peacefully enough. Everything changed in the summer of 1817—that's when the first noises began. It started with knocking sounds on the doors and walls late at night. The family noticed strange-looking animals roaming the property. Next came the sounds of chains dragging across the floors followed by choking sounds. This intensified over the year until the Bells were no longer able to withstand the frightening occurrences. John confided to his friend and neighbor James Johnson about the terrors that were lurking in his home. Johnson tried doing an investigation and experienced these inexplicable occurrences himself. As time went on the spiritual presence in the Bells' home began to speak, then to sing! The voice answered with various names when asked who it was. Eventually the spirit said it was Kate

Batts. Kate had been a neighbor who had lived and died in a cave on the Bells' property. She was an eccentric and unpleasant person whom many of the mountain people had suspected of being a Witch. That's when the supernatural force became known as "The Bells' Witch, Kate."

Periodically stones would pelt the family home or even be thrown at guests. Everything began to suggest poltergeist activity centering around one daughter, Elizabeth. The young girl was tormented with slaps and assaults by the spirit. John Bell was the second target of Kate's anger. The Witch would laugh at and threaten John, even saying that she would kill him! The attacks became more serious, ending in the family patriarch being unable to swallow or speak.

The entrance to Bell Witch Cave

75

Kate was heard to say, "I've got him this time, he'll never get out of that bed again." This incident led to Tennessee being the only state to allow supernatural causes to be an acceptable cause of death.

Kate claimed to have given John a dose of some dark liquid from a bottle by his bedside. The Witch then sang drunken and bawdy songs and cursed while he died of convulsions. The liquid was examined and found to be arsenic. Even as John's coffin was placed in his grave the voice was heard with its insults and taunts.

Strangely the only family member Kate seemed to like was Mrs. Lucy Bell, old John's young wife. Kate announced that she would leave the family after the death. She was true to this promise for many years. When Kate returned, only Lucy—by then ailing and very elderly—and two of her sons were still living on the farm. Neighbors who visited the sick woman witnessed materializations and heard Kate's voice. To this day many feel the spirit of Kate Batts still lurks in the area. A female figure is said to materialize along Highway 41 close to where the Bell Witch Cave is located. In 1975 a descendant of John and Lucy named Carney Bell claimed that Kate led him to find a lost and overgrown family gravestone.

A tall, imposing historical marker can be found near Adams dedicated to the Bell family and the famous hauntings. Modern-day paranormal investigators have recorded voices and other phenomena on film in the Bell Witch's Cave and ghost hunters have posted the videos on YouTube. The Bell Witch cave is open for tours. It is located at 430 Keysburg Road in Adams, TN, 37010. The phone number is 615-896-3055. There is a website with details about the annual Fall Festival, where a play about this authentic story of the Bell Witch is presented. See BellWitchFestival.com for more information.

—ESTHER NEUMEIER

SPRINGFIELD, Jan. 27. — [Special.] Mr. Joel E. Ball, of this place, died yesterday. He occupied a prominent place on the Board of the Cumberland Baptist Association, and was a very clear-headed, highly respected citizen, being almost an octogenarian.

Nashville death notice for Joel Egbert Bell, the last surviving child of John and Lucy Bell.

SUNRISE, SUNSET
The Magical Rhythms of Every Day

IN EVERYDAY life most people are beholden to the clock. You have to catch a bus, be at work, get on a phone call, all on a particular schedule set at times beyond your control. Twice a year the clocks change for Daylight Saving Time—by an act of bizarre magic, an hour's worth of time vanishes or appears. When that happens, the whole country wakes up groggy and disoriented. It takes most people at least a week to adjust to a new schedule: they're no longer hungry at mealtime and daylight comes and goes at all the *wrong* times.

But the power of the clock is incontrovertible. The bus doesn't care that you're groggy from waking up an hour earlier—all it knows is that it makes its stop when the clock says 7:15. Nonetheless, when you wake and check your phone to see the time is somehow wrong, it becomes obvious how arbitrary clock time is. The clock only measures the passage of time by common convention and sometimes that convention bizarrely and abruptly changes.

The Sun rises and sets today the same way it did yesterday but the clock doesn't keep in sync with it. Just by looking at a clock, you have no actual way of knowing what time it feels like in the world outside—whether it is light or dark, early or late. These things change with the seasons and the passing of each day in a way that clocks simply can't track. There are two ways of measuring time—one in the world and one in a microchip. Most days, people don't stop to think about how separate those two are, but if you stop and pay attention, they come apart in a jarring way.

Witchcraft places great emphasis on the cycles of nature. Witches work with the changing of the seasons, the phases of the Moon and the passage of the planets through the great wheel of the Zodiac. All of these are ways of measuring time, attuning yourself directly to the rhythms of the divinely ensouled world. Everyone has to track mundane time using the days, weeks and months on the calendar but ultimately, those things are nothing more than words on a page put in place by a collective agreement. They're not *in* the world. By contrast, Witches track sacred time by observing the constant and recurring change in the

77

world around them. They watch the Moon grow fat and thin again and they observe the first snowfall of Winter and the first flowers of Spring.

One of the most important rhythms in natural magic is that of sunrise and sunset in each passing day. The world measures mundane time by the clock and there is nothing you can do to control the ordinary clock-time obligations you have in the world—the bus comes whether you want it to or not. But there is also a sacred time that moves through every day and doesn't answer to social conventions. Every evening, the Sun dies and travels through the Underworld and every morning it is reborn.

One easy way to keep in tune with this sacred time is to keep track of the Sun's passage through the sky. Keep alarms on your phone and set them to go off each day—one at sunrise, one at astronomical midday and one at

sunset. When these alarms chime—no matter what you're doing—stop, go outside and notice the Sun. Take a moment to breathe, forget about clock time and allow yourself to feel the ongoing dance of Earth and Sun. For a moment, dissolve into the sacred.

This practice is certainly not new. Ritual celebration of the Sun's daily journey is found throughout the world. In modern magic it's perhaps best known in the solar adorations of Aleister Crowley's *Liber Resh*, which are performed at sunrise, noon, sunset and midnight. But observing the sacred rhythms of the Sun doesn't need to be nearly as involved as Crowley's rituals. You can keep a small, minimalistic practice aimed at maintaining mindfulness of the Sun's passage, a connection to the Earth's daily cycle that has nothing to do with the hours showing on a clock. You can also do more, making

an offering or saying a few words to follow the Sun on its journey—but it is enough simply to turn toward the Sun and take a few deep breaths.

Simple though it is, the observation of sacred time is one of the most important foundational elements of Witchcraft. It keeps the practitioner in connection with the ongoing rhythms of the land and the slow change of the Sun as each day grows longer or shorter. Every morning, you can watch in rapture as the Sun is born. Every evening, you solemnly witness its death. In these acts, the central mysteries of magic are ever present, allowing sacred time to take precedence over the mundane time set by the clock.

In his novel *To a God Unknown*, John Steinbeck describes a man who lives at the westernmost edge of California and makes sacrifices every night to the setting Sun. This nightly ritual allows him to identify himself with the Sun and to experience the mystery of its death as it disappears over the Pacific: "I have said to myself, 'The sun is life. I give life to life'—'I make a symbol of the sun's death'...it is for me. In the moment, I am the sun. Do you see ?"

This passage gets at the heart of something important and magical. Steinbeck's character sees the power inherent in the sunset and gives himself over to it, allowing himself to be consumed each night in the mystery of the Sun's death. He lives wholly in sacred time, in the eternal recurrence of the Sun's death and rebirth. You might not have the luxury of spending all your time in the sacred—you still have to show up at work and answer to the clock. But by setting yourself apart for sunrise and sunset, you can still carry the sacred with you every day.

—JACK CHANECK

79

2024 SUNRISE AND SUNSET TIMES

Providence—San Francisco—Sydney—London

	Sunrise				Sunset			
	Prov	SF	Syd	Lon	Prov	SF	Syd	Lon
Jan 5	7:14 AM	7:26 AM	5:51 AM	8:06 AM	4:28 PM	5:03 PM	8:08 PM	4:05 PM
15	7:11 AM	7:24 AM	6:00 AM	8:00 AM	4:38 PM	5:13 PM	8:07 PM	4:19 PM
25	7:05 AM	7:19 AM	6:09 AM	7:50 AM	4:50 PM	5:24 PM	8:04 PM	4:35 PM
Feb 5	6:55 AM	7:11 AM	6:20 AM	7:34 AM	5:04 PM	5:36 PM	7:56 PM	4:55 PM
15	6:42 AM	7:00 AM	6:30 AM	7:16 AM	5:17 PM	5:47 PM	7:47 PM	5:13 PM
25	6:28 AM	6:47 AM	6:39 AM	6:56 AM	5:29 PM	5:58 PM	7:36 PM	5:31 PM
Mar 5	6:14 AM	6:35 AM	6:47 AM	6:36 AM	5:40 PM	6:07 PM	7:25 PM	5:47 PM
15	6:57 AM	7:20 AM	6:55 AM	6:14 AM	6:51 PM	7:16 PM	7:12 PM	6:04 PM
25	6:40 AM	7:05 AM	7:03 AM	5:51 AM	7:03 PM	7:25 PM	6:58 PM	6:21 PM
Apr 5	6:21 AM	6:49 AM	7:11 AM	6:27 AM	7:15 PM	7:35 PM	6:43 PM	7:40 PM
15	6:05 AM	6:34 AM	6:18 AM	6:05 AM	7:26 PM	7:44 PM	5:31 PM	7:56 PM
25	5:50 AM	6:21 AM	6:26 AM	5:44 AM	7:37 PM	7:54 PM	5:19 PM	8:13 PM
May 5	5:37 AM	6:09 AM	6:33 AM	5:25 AM	7:47 PM	8:03 PM	5:09 PM	8:29 PM
15	5:26 AM	6:00 AM	6:41 AM	5:09 AM	7:58 PM	8:12 PM	5:01 PM	8:45 PM
25	5:18 AM	5:53 AM	6:48 AM	4:56 AM	8:07 PM	8:20 PM	4:55 PM	8:59 PM
June 5	5:12 AM	5:49 AM	6:54 AM	4:47 AM	8:16 PM	8:27 PM	4:52 PM	9:11 PM
15	5:11 AM	5:48 AM	6:59 AM	4:44 AM	8:21 PM	8:32 PM	4:52 PM	9:18 PM
25	5:13 AM	5:50 AM	7:01 AM	4:45 AM	8:23 PM	8:34 PM	4:54 PM	9:20 PM
July 5	5:18 AM	5:55 AM	7:01 AM	4:52 AM	8:22 PM	8:33 PM	4:58 PM	9:17 PM
15	5:25 AM	6:01 AM	6:58 AM	5:02 AM	8:17 PM	8:29 PM	5:03 PM	9:09 PM
25	5:34 AM	6:09 AM	6:53 AM	5:15 AM	8:09 PM	8:22 PM	5:10 PM	8:57 PM
Aug 5	5:45 AM	6:18 AM	6:44 AM	5:32 AM	7:57 PM	8:12 PM	5:17 PM	8:39 PM
15	5:55 AM	6:26 AM	6:34 AM	5:47 AM	7:43 PM	8:00 PM	5:24 PM	8:20 PM
25	6:05 AM	6:35 AM	6:23 AM	6:03 AM	7:28 PM	7:46 PM	5:31 PM	8:00 PM
Sept 5	6:17 AM	6:44 AM	6:09 AM	6:21 AM	7:10 PM	7:30 PM	5:39 PM	7:35 PM
15	6:27 AM	6:53 AM	5:55 AM	6:37 AM	6:53 PM	7:15 PM	5:45 PM	7:12 PM
25	6:37 AM	7:01 AM	5:41 AM	6:53 AM	6:35 PM	6:59 PM	5:52 PM	6:49 PM
Oct 5	6:48 AM	7:10 AM	5:27 AM	7:09 AM	6:18 PM	6:44 PM	5:59 PM	6:27 PM
15	6:59 AM	7:19 AM	6:14 AM	7:26 AM	6:02 PM	6:30 PM	7:07 PM	6:05 PM
25	7:11 AM	7:29 AM	6:03 AM	7:43 AM	5:47 PM	6:17 PM	7:15 PM	5:44 PM
Nov 5	6:24 AM	6:40 AM	5:52 AM	7:02 AM	4:33 PM	5:05 PM	7:25 PM	4:24 PM
15	6:36 AM	6:51 AM	5:44 AM	7:19 AM	4:23 PM	4:56 PM	7:35 PM	4:09 PM
25	6:48 AM	7:01 AM	5:39 AM	7:36 AM	4:16 PM	4:51 PM	7:44 PM	3:58 PM
Dec 5	6:58 AM	7:11 AM	5:38 AM	7:50 AM	4:13 PM	4:49 PM	7:53 PM	3:52 PM
15	7:07 AM	7:19 AM	5:39 AM	8:00 AM	4:14 PM	4:51 PM	8:01 PM	3:50 PM
25	7:12 AM	7:24 AM	5:44 AM	8:06 AM	4:19 PM	4:56 PM	8:06 PM	3:55 PM

Prov=Providence; SF=San Francisco; Syd=Sydney; Lon=London
Times are presented in the standard time of the geographical location, using the current time zone of that place.

Window on the Weather

It started with a whisper in the tropics, the warning signs of a powerful change in the climate. El Niño has arrived, and with it the 11-year solar maximum. The eastern Pacific Ocean became warmer, and the traditional agricultural communities of Peru, Ecuador, and Colombia felt its effects. The heat waves and droughts lead to crop failures and diseases, leaving many without food security. Across North America and western Europe, the opposite is occurring, and crop yields are bound to increase. In addition, El Niño brings powerful storms, which cause damage to coastal cities closer to the equator. But the impact of this unusual combination of events did not stop at the edge of the Caribbean. Parts of South America, Asia, and Africa are feeling the impact of El Niño and the 11-year solar minimum as well. In India, increased temperatures are making it difficult for farmers to maintain their crops. Meanwhile, in Southeast Asia, the reduced precipitation is linked to an increase in dry soil conditions. The arrival of these weather conditions presents a unique challenge to many parts of the world. It's a call to action to find ways to protect ourselves, our families, and our environment from the impact of natural variance. Fortunately, people around the world are beginning to realize the importance of taking action to protect ourselves as stewards of the planet.

SPRING

MARCH 2024 Historically, El Niño conditions in North America bring warmer temperatures and wetter conditions to the southern regions of the continent. This in turn can lead to more severe tornado season storms in the southern states, as well as increased flood risks for many areas. During 11-year solar maximums, the El Niño effect can become more pronounced, leading to more extreme weather events. The economic impact of this can be seen in areas with large agricultural industries that rely on consistent growing conditions and rainfall. The effects of El Niño on climate patterns and the resulting economic impacts can vary from region to region. In places such as the Pacific Northwest, colder winters are expected due to the El Niño effect, potentially leading to an extended ski season. Meanwhile, in regions such as the Southwest, warmer temperatures and more frequent droughts could have serious implications for agricultural production. In the Midwest, increased rainfall could lead to more flooding risks, disrupting transportation and leading to higher insurance costs.

APRIL 2024 Springtime in North America is a season of transition. As winter gradually fades away, spring brings warmer temperatures, budding flowers, and increased precipitation. However, the arrival of spring can also have an impact on weather patterns across the continent. El Niño conditions—an event characterized by ocean-atmosphere interactions in the tropical Pacific Ocean—can have a major influence on the climate of North America, especially during the spring months. El Niño creates warmer temperatures and more moisture in the atmosphere, resulting in higher than normal rainfall across much of the continent. This can have profound implications on the tornado season. Typically, spring tornado activity begins in March and continues into April, but with El Niño conditions, tornado activity often starts earlier in the year as more moisture is available in the atmosphere during this time. The number and intensity of tornadoes tend to increase. This can be particularly hazardous in the south-central United States, where there is already a higher than normal risk of tornado activity. El Niño also has an impact on spring snowfall. With warmer temperatures, heavy snowfalls are less likely and ski resorts may suffer a significant shortfall in revenue.

MAY 2024 Generally, May weather across North America is characterized by warm temperatures, increased precipitation, and increased thunderstorm activity. El Niño at the solar maximum may bring warmer temperatures and increased precipitation, but the overall effects on tornadoes will largely depend on other factors such as the strength of upper-level winds, atmospheric moisture, and instability of the environment. Tornadoes are most common in the spring, when warm, humid air from the Gulf of Mexico clashes with cold Arctic air. El Niño can enhance this clash by increasing the jet stream, which increases both the severity of the storm system and the potential for tornadoes to form. However, the recent solar maximum could bring cooler temperatures and increased stability, which could decrease tornado activity across the northern plains, while the Ohio valley and mid-Atlantic states see increased activity. Above normal rainfall is also likely through New England and the Pacific Northwest

SUMMER

JUNE 2024 Scientists believe that El Niño is linked to sunspot activity. Sunspots are dark spots on the surface of the sun which typically appear in cycles of 11 years. During a solar maximum, sunspots occur more frequently and the sun's magnetic field strength increases which can cause increased global temperatures. While this is beneficial in some areas of the world, it often causes high tempera-

tures and dry conditions in the northern hemisphere during June. During an El Niño event, the warming of the central and eastern Pacific Ocean leads to far-reaching impacts on world climate patterns. In terms of weather, El Niño causes higher temperatures and drier conditions in Northern Europe and the United States. For example, during the summers of 1997 and 1998, 11-year solar maximums coincided with El Niño events, resulting in higher temperatures and drought in parts of the United States and Mexico. In northern Europe, temperatures were also above average in June of 1997 and 1998. The impacts of El Niño on weather patterns during 11-year solar maximums can also be seen in Asia. During the most recent solar maximum in 2013, the summer was very dry in eastern China due to high air pressure caused by El Niño.

JULY 2024 Thunderstorms occur when warm, moist air rises rapidly and cools, forming cumulonimbus clouds. These clouds can produce lightning, hail, and strong winds. During El Niño events, the jet stream shifts southward and brings more moisture to the southern states. This increased moisture makes thunderstorms more likely to form. The 11-year solar maximums also have an effect on thunderstorm activity in the United States. During these periods, the sun's activity is at its peak and the Earth's climate is affected. Solar radiation heats up the atmosphere, which can cause air to rise faster and create more thunderstorms. The effects of El Niño and 11-year solar maximums on thunderstorm activity in the United States vary from region to region. Areas that have historically experienced greater thunderstorm activity in July during El Niño events include the Gulf Coast, the Southeast, the Midwest, and parts of the Southwest. These regions tend to experience more moisture from El Niño, which can lead to more thunderstorms. Additionally, these areas may be more prone to severe weather events due to their geography or climate.

AUGUST 2024 El Niño events can have significant impact on climate and weather patterns across the United States. During these events, the jet stream is suppressed to the south, which can cause lower temperatures yet higher humidity in some areas across the country. Additionally, the westerly winds aloft in the tropics can create a wind shear that suppresses the formation and intensification of hurricanes. This can lead to below-average hurricane activity during the season. The effects of El Niño events are felt in other ways as well. The increased moisture in the atmosphere can lead to above-average rainfall in some areas of the United States. This can be beneficial for agricultural production in certain regions, but it can also lead to flooding. El Niño events can also impact global temperatures. While the jet stream is suppressed to the south, warmer air from the tropics is able to move further north than usual. This can cause temperatures to rise in some areas, leading to an overall increase in global temperatures.

AUTUMN

SEPTEMBER 2024 According to data from the National Oceanic and Atmospheric Administration (NOAA), El Niño events have been associated with warmer temperatures and higher precipitation levels in some areas of the country during September. In the southeastern United States, for example, El Niño events have been linked to an increase in the number of days with temperatures above 90°F, plus an increase in rainfall in that part of the country and farther north along the eastern seaboard. This can lead to flooding in low-lying areas, which can cause property damage and disruption to daily life. In the western United States, El Niño events can lead to an increased risk of wildfires due to the dry conditions that accompany the ENSO events. El Niño can have a significant impact on the climate and weather patterns of the United States into September. It is important that we continue to monitor these events and understand how they will affect our environment. By doing so, we can better prepare for any potential impacts that may arise.

OCTOBER 2024 An El Niño event's impact on the United States can extend into the fall months. During such, the jet stream flows through southern states, allowing warmer air from the tropics to move further north than usual. This can lead to above-average temperatures there, while farther north below-average temperatures are likely. The effects of El Niño on precipitation can vary greatly depending on the region. In some areas of the country, El Niño events can lead to above-average rainfall and snowfall. For example, during the 1997-1998 El Niño event, California experienced an unusually wet October with higher than average precipitation. On the other hand, areas such as the Midwest may experience below-average rainfall. During the 2015-2016 El Niño event, the Southwest experienced above-average temperatures while the Northwest and Northeast were cooler than normal. Similarly, the Northwest and Northeast experienced above-average rainfall while the Southwest was drier than usual.

NOVEMBER 2024 The jet stream, still suppressed to the south, will cause lower temperatures yet higher humidity in some areas across the country. Additionally, the westerly winds aloft in the tropics can create a wind shear that suppresses the formation of hurricanes as that season ends. The increased moisture in the atmosphere due to the ongoing El Niño can lead to above-average rainfall in some areas of the United States, beneficial for the harvest in certain regions. In particular, the Midwest and Northeast regions of the United States are prone to flooding during El Niño years. In November 1998, for example, flooding occurred in the Ohio Valley due to heavy rains from El Niño. The increased mois-

ture in the atmosphere can also lead to an increase in lake effect snowfall. In November 2002, lake effect snowfall was observed in the Great Lakes region due to such conditions. This can be beneficial for ski resorts and other businesses that rely on snowfall. El Niño events can also bring an increase in wildfire activity due to the dry conditions that they can cause. In November 2015, for example, El Niño was linked to the devastating wildfires in California.

WINTER

DECEMBER 2024 The ongoing El Niño event and weakening 11-year solar cycle will regulate early winter weather patterns across the United States during December. During such times, the jet stream is suppressed to the south, causing lower temperatures yet higher precipitation in some areas across the country. This can lead to heavy snowfall regionally, while other places may experience flooding due to the increased moisture in the atmosphere. In December 2015, El Niño conditions caused above-average snowfall across the northern United States. The Midwest and Northeast saw particularly heavy snowfall, with some areas receiving up to 30 inches of snow. This was due to the increased storm frequency, as well as the colder temperatures brought about by the jet stream being suppressed to the south. In addition to snowfall, El Niño events can bring about increased flooding risks. El Niño can also impact temperatures across the United States during December. The warmer air from the tropics can move further north than usual, resulting in higher temperatures. This can be beneficial for agricultural production where rainfall persists, but can also lead to an increased risk of wildfires in California and the interior southwest.

JANUARY 2025 During moderate El Niño events, when the 11-year solar cycle is weakening, temperatures across the United States can become unusually warm. This can lead to reduced snowfall in some areas and increased flooding in others. In January 2017, for example, an El Niño event combined with a weakening 11-year solar cycle caused temperatures to be higher than normal across the United States. This resulted in reduced snowfall in some areas, such as the Midwest and the Great Lakes region, while other areas experienced more rainfall than usual. In particular, the Pacific Northwest saw an increase in precipitation due to the combination of El Niño and the weakening 11-year solar cycle. The effects of El Niño events can vary by region. In the Southeast, for instance, that combination can cause temperatures to become unusually cold, leading to heavy snowfall in some areas, such as the Appalachian Mountains. In January 2014 such conditions caused temperatures to drop to below freezing

in some parts of the Southeast, and in January 2017 caused flooding in parts of the Midwest and the Great Lakes region.

FEBRUARY 2025 In recent years, moderate El Niños have coincided with weakening 11-year solar cycles, leading to above-normal snowfall in certain regions. In 2011, those events resulted in record-breaking snowfall in the Midwest and Northeast, causing travel disruptions and school closings. Similarly, in 2015, another moderate El Niño combined with a weakening solar cycle led to record-breaking snowfall in the Rockies and Plains states. An El Niño event can also increase tornado activity across the United States during February. In 2008, it resulted in an unusually active tornado season, with more than 1,000 tornadoes reported across the country. Similar conditions in 2014 produced more than 1,200 tornadoes. In addition to increased snowfall and tornado activity, moderate El Niño events combined with weakening 11-year solar cycles can also lead to flooding in California. In 1998, record-breaking rainfall and flooding across the state, causing billions of dollars in damage. Similarly, in 2010, another moderate El Niño caused devastating flooding in California, resulting in more than $1 billion in damages. Overall, El Niño events, combined with weakening 11-year solar cycles, can have a significant impact on the weather across the United States. During February, these conditions can lead to increased snowfall, tornado activity, and flooding in some areas.

Living off The Land

A Hedge Witches' Survival Guide

Rising grocery prices combined with interruption in the supply chain of the availability of foods makes the prospect of wildcrafting appealing to those who follow the Old Ways and strive to live the magical life. Wildcrafting is the practice of finding food as well as cosmetic and personal care items available for the taking in nature. A treasure trove of these can be found growing in forests as well as in gardens, vacant lots and along roadsides. Nutritious and tasty salads, cooked greens, desserts, soups and more can be prepared by foraging for these surprisingly plentiful free foods.

When on a tour of Ireland in the 1990's a tour guide told a group of how good nettle soup was while pointing out the plants growing by the road. She added that many of those in need still made it often as a good and filling lunch or dinner. The travel group was so intrigued by this that she arranged to have the chef at the hotel serve nettle soup for dinner the next night. It was indeed very tasty!

Whether for reasons of economic need or just to enjoy the natural foods and remedies, trying a bit of wildcrafting adds a new dimension of magic and power to daily living. Of course some plants are naturally toxic or polluted so caution is advised. A salad of poison ivy leaves would hardly be a good choice! A little study of the local landscape can point out many suitable options to select from.

87

For example, aside from nettles, dandelions grow nearly everywhere and are very tasty when prepared properly. In the desert Southwest of the United States cactus plants can be harvested and prepared as an excellent food source. Acorns are extremely nutritious and readily available in many regions. They offer a healthy and convenient addition to many menu choices and are a good way to begin wildcrafting.

Acorns are readily identified. They are the seeds of the oak trees, which grow throughout North America and Europe. Acorns can be easily collected from September through November when they fall from the trees making them accessible to deer, squirrels and resourceful humans. About every five years oak trees and other plants will have a *mast*—a botanical term meaning a bumper crop, when a large number of especially nutritious seeds are produced. This benefits foraging wildlife, plant propagation—and hungry humans.

A glance at the divine and magical connections with wildcrafted plants can add to the mystique of this practice. For example, acorns are sacred to the Norse Goddess Freya. A patroness of crops, she often styles her hair in an acorn shaped coiffure

When gathering acorns, look for brown, fully mature ones that still have their caps. Avoid acorns without caps because they are more susceptible to infestation by worms, bugs, etc. Green acorns are not yet mature and they are inedible. Caution: All acorns contain bitter and irritating substances called tannins. These must be leached out before the nuts can be eaten. Consuming tannins can cause nausea and constipation, but with just a bit of patience and time the tannins are easily removed.

Preparation of food grade acorns:
1. Start by rinsing the acorns in cool water. Place them in a bowl and cover with fresh water. Toss out floating acorns as these have gone bad.
2. Place the acorns in a colander and run them under the tap in order to dislodge any loose dirt or pests.
3. Set the colander aside and let the acorns air-dry.
4. Remove the shells and caps from

88

your acorns. Use a nutcracker or a hammer. Remove tannins from the raw acorns. Below is a time-tested method. Although, some folks suggest just placing the acorns in a basket and suspending it in a stream for several days instead.

How to Remove Tannins from Acorns (Leaching)

1. Start by boiling two pots of water. Drop the raw, shell-less acorns into one pot and boil until the water is the color of strong tea.
2. Strain the nuts through a colander and drop the strained nuts into the second pot of boiling water. Discard the dark water from the first pot, then refill it and bring the water to a boil again.
3. Repeat the process without interruption (do not let the acorns cool or dry out) until the water boils clear. This may take an hour or more.
4. Alternatively, you can merely soak the raw acorns in cold water to leach the tannins out. Just change the water when it turnsa dark color. This may take several days.

How to Grind Acorns for Cooking

1. Spread tannin-free acorns to dry on cookie sheets in a warm place. When dry, grind a few acorns at a time using a blender.
2. Spread the ground acorns to dry on cookie sheets, then grind again.
3. Repeat until you have a dry flour that has a cornmeal-like texture.

Once you have prepared the acorn flour it is ready to use. Here is a delicious recipe to try.

Acorn Pancakes Recipe

Ingredients:
One egg
1 tsp. olive oil
1 tsp. honey or sugar
½ cup acorn flour
½ cup cornmeal
½ cup whole wheat or all-purpose white flour
2 tsp. baking powder
½ tsp. salt
½ cup milk

Instructions:

Break egg into bowl and add all ingredients, beating to create a batter. If batter is too thick, thin with additional milk. Pour batter onto hot, greased griddle and cook slowly until brown. Flip to brown opposite side. Serve with butter and maple syrup or your favorite marmalade or jam. Enjoy!

—MARINA BRYONY

the fixed stars

Albireo

Jewels in the Mouth of the Swan

EACH YEAR *The Witches' Almanac* features a different fixed star. Fixed stars have been referenced as important fine points, used in astrological interpretations since the Middle Ages and before. Look at the Sun, Moon or a planet placed within a small orb of just a degree or two to understand the star's full potential. The impact seems to have the most marked effect when a fixed star is conjunct one of the planets from Jupiter out to Pluto. This year's choice is Albireo, a double or binary star currently located

at about 1 degree Aquarius 40'. (Fixed is a bit of a misnomer. The stars actually do move, but very slowly, just over a degree in a century.) Albireo is located 430 light years from Earth and is 230 times brighter than our Sun. It appears as the brightest star in the constellation Cygnus, the Swan. Close observation with a good telescope will reveal that it is actually binary, that is two stars orbiting each other, a larger topaz yellow star and a smaller, dimmer sapphire blue star. This double star is located in the

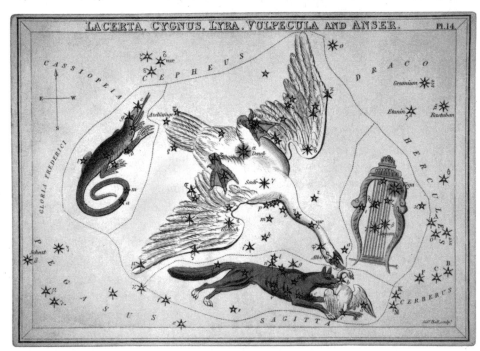

90

head of the Swan, often described as the jewel in the bird's beak. Esoteric astrologers have related Albireo (the name is derived from the Greek word Ornis) to a song, "The Dying Swan." It has the nature of Venus combined with Mercury. This gives Albireo the qualities of idealism, refinement, gentility, neatness and beauty. It is said to bring beneficence in despair when active in a horoscope. During 2024 Pluto will enter Aquarius and will transit within orb of Albireo for most of the year. Its influence will intertwine with event charts throughout the entire time. It will also impact the natal charts of children born with Pluto in the early degrees of Aquarius.

Times when world events and human consciousness can be influenced by this fixed star are December 6–7, 2024, when Venus conjoins Albireo, and January 27–28, 2025 when Mercury conjoins it. Those are times when world events and human consciousness can be influenced by this fixed star. Some possibilities include new behavioral trends and fashion statements surfacing as well as significant musical and artistic expression. Materialistic concerns can motivate many too. A subtle hedonism is likely to prevail. There might be a significant scandal involving a celebrity relationship surfacing near these dates as well.

Those born on January 20 of any year will have Albireo conjunct the natal Sun. Notable nativities born on this date whose lives reflect the influence of this star include Nikki Haley, Buzz Aldrin, Kellyanne Conway and Bill Maher. In other birth charts look for natal placements located from 0 to 2 degrees of Aquarius. Here is a guide to the influences Albireo indicates when conjunct a natal planet or luminary.

With the Moon: good health, honor, happy home, joyful social connections

The Sun: gifts, legacies, helpful friends

Mercury: popularity, conformity, music and art appreciation

Venus: materialistic values, love of fancy clothing, pleasure seeking, artistic and musical

Mars: extroverted display, love of ease, luxury, superficial or insincere

Jupiter: social advancement, success, religious outlook

Saturn: studious, serious, reserved, stressful home life

Uranus: timid, economical, psychic ability, occult studies

Neptune: easily influenced and led by others, visionary, addiction prone

Pluto: energetic, sharp mind, prefers an independent business or career direction

The deeper nuances emitted by this fixed star might be perceived within the meaning of *The Dying Swan* ballet. Written for Anna Pavlova, Mikhail Fokine told dance critic Arnold Haskell in 1934 that the meaning of *The Dying Swan* ballet was not to showcase technique, but to "create the symbol of the everlasting struggle in this life and all that is mortal." This observation seems to particularly resonate with the message of the transit of Pluto in the early degrees of Aquarius when conjoining Albireo. In addition to the famous ballet, the Dying Swan theme was also an inspiration for Tennyson in a poem. Astrologers who practice esoteric astrology are invited to explore these sources while interpreting the fixed star Albireo.

—DIKKI-JO MULLEN

The Dying Swan
By Alfred Lord Tennyson

I

The plain was grassy, wild and bare,
Wide, wild, and open to the air,
Which had built up everywhere
An under-roof of doleful gray.
With an inner voice the river ran,
Adown it floated a dying swan,
And loudly did lament.
It was the middle of the day.
Ever the weary wind went on,
And took the reed-tops as it went.

II

Some blue peaks in the distance rose,
And white against the cold-white sky,
Shone out their crowning snows.
One willow over the water wept,
And shook the wave as the wind did sigh;
Above in the wind was the swallow,
Chasing itself at its own wild will,
And far thro' the marish green and still
The tangled water-courses slept,
Shot over with purple, and green, and yellow.

III

The wild swan's death-hymn took the soul
Of that waste place with joy
Hidden in sorrow: at first to the ear
The warble was low, and full and clear;
And floating about the under-sky,
Prevailing in weakness, the coronach stole
Sometimes afar, and sometimes anear;
But anon her awful jubilant voice,
With a music strange and manifold,
Flow'd forth on a carol free and bold;
As when a mighty people rejoice
With shawms, and with cymbals, and harps of gold,
And the tumult of their acclaim is roll'd
Thro' the open gates of the city afar,
To the shepherd who watcheth the evening star.
And the creeping mosses and clambering weeds,
And the willow-branches hoar and dank,
And the wavy swell of the soughing reeds,
And the wave-worn horns of the echoing bank,
And the silvery marish-flowers that throng
The desolate creeks and pools among,
Were flooded over with eddying song.

The Court Cards

NOW MANY beautiful things may be cut out of and pasted on paper! Thus a castle was cut out and pasted, so large that it filled a whole table, and it was painted as if it were built of red stones. It had a shining copper roof, it had towers and a draw-bridge, water in the canals just like plate glass, for it was plate-glass, and in the highest tower stood a wooden watchman. He had a trumpet, but he did not blow it.

The whole belonged to a little boy, whose name was William. He raised the draw-bridge himself and let it down again, made his tin soldiers march over it, opened the castle gate and looked into the large and elegant drawing-room, where all the court cards of a pack—Hearts, Diamonds, Clubs, and Spades—hung in frames on the walls, like pictures in real drawing rooms. The kings held each a scepter, and wore crowns; the queens wore veils flowing down over their shoulders, and in their hands they held a flower or a fan; the knaves had halberds and nodding plumes.

One evening the little boy peeped through the open castle gate, to catch a glimpse of the court cards in the drawing room, and it seemed to him that the kings saluted him with their scepters, that the Queen of Spades swung the golden tulip which she held in her hand, that the Queen of Hearts lifted her fan, and that all four queens graciously recognized him. He drew a little nearer, in order to see better, and that made him hit his head against the castle so that it shook. Then all the four knaves of Hearts, Diamonds, Clubs, and Spades, raised their halberds, to warn him that he must not try to get in that way.

The little boy understood the hint, and gave a friendly nod; he nodded again, and then said: "Say something!" but the knaves did not say a word. However, the third time be nodded, the Knave of Hearts sprang out of the

94

card, and placed himself in the middle of the floor.

"What is your name?" the knave asked the little boy. "You have clear eyes and good teeth, but your hands are dirty: you do not wash them often enough!"

Now this was rather coarse language, but, of course, not much politeness can be expected from a knave. He is only a common fellow.

"My name is William," said the little boy, "and the castle is mine, and you are my Knave of Hearts!"

"No, I am not. I am my king's and my queen's knave, not yours!" said the Knave of Hearts. "I am not obliged to stay here. I can get down off the card, and out of the frame too, and so can my gracious king and queen, even more easily than I. We can go out into the wide world, but that is such a wearisome march; we have grown tired of it; it is more convenient, more easy, more agreeable, to be sitting in the cards, and just to be ourselves!"

"Have all of you really been human beings once?" asked little William.

"Human beings!" repeated the Knave of Hearts. "Yes, we have; but not so good as we ought to have been! Please now light a little wax candle (I like a red one best, for that is the color of my king and queen); then I will tell the lord of the castle—I think you said you were the lord of the castle, did you not?—our whole history; but for goodness' sake, don't interrupt me, for if I speak, it must be done without any interruption whatever. I am in a great hurry! Do you see my king, I mean the King of Hearts? He is the oldest of the four kings there, for he was born first,—born with a golden crown and a golden apple. He began to rule at once. His queen was born with a golden fan; that she still has. They both were very agreeably situated, even from infancy. They did not have to go to school, they could play the whole day, build castles, and knock them down, marshal tin soldiers for battle, and play with dolls. When they asked for buttered bread, then there was butter on both sides of the bread, and powdered brown sugar, too, nicely spread over it. It was the good old time, and was called the Golden Age; but they grew tired of it, and so did I. Then the King of Diamonds took the reins of government!"

The knave said nothing more. Little William waited to hear something further, but not a syllable was uttered; so presently he asked,—"Well, and then?"

The Knave of Hearts did not answer; he stood up straight, silent, bold, and stiff, his eyes fixed upon the burning wax candle. Little William nodded; he nodded again, but no reply. Then he turned to the Knave of Diamonds; and when he had nodded to him three times, up he sprang out of the card, in the middle of the floor, and uttered only one single word,—"Wax candle!"

Little William understood what he meant, and immediately lighted a red candle, and placed it before him. Then the Knave of Diamonds presented arms, for that is a token of respect, and said:—"Then the King of Diamonds succeeded to the throne! He was a king with a pane of glass on his breast; also the queen had a pane of glass on her breast, so that people could look right into her. For the rest, they were formed like other human beings, and were so agreeable and so handsome, that a monument was erected in honor of them, which stood for seven years without falling. Properly speaking, it should have stood forever, for so it was intended; but from some unknown reasons, it fell." Then the Knave of Diamonds presented arms, out of respect for his king, and he looked fixedly on his red wax candle.

But now at once, without any nod or invitation from little William, the Knave of Clubs stepped out, grave and proud, like the stork that struts with such a dignified air over the green meadow. The black clover-leaf in the corner of the card flew like a bird beyond the knave, and then flew back again, and stuck itself where it had been sticking before.

And without waiting for his wax candle, the Knave of Clubs spoke:—"Not all get butter on both sides of the bread, and brown powdered sugar on that. My king and queen did not get it. They had to go to school, and learn what they had not learnt before. They also had a pane of glass on their breasts, but nobody looked through it, except to see if there was not something wrong with their works inside, in order to find, if possible,

some reason for giving them a scolding! I know it; I have served my king and queen all my life-time; I know everything about them, and obey their commands. They bid me say nothing more to-night. 1 keep silent, therefore, and present arms!"

But little William was a kind-hearted boy, so he lighted a candle for this knave also, a shining white one, white like snow. No sooner was the candle lighted, than the Knave of Spades appeared in the middle of the drawing-room. He came hurriedly; yet he limped, as if he had a sore leg. Indeed, it had once been broken, and he had had, moreover, many ups and down in his life. He spoke as follows:—

"My brother knaves have each got a candle, and I shall also get one; I know that. But if we poor knaves have so much honor, our kings and queens must have thrice as much. Now, it is proper that my King of Spades and my Queen of Spades should have four candles to gladden them. An additional honor ought to be conferred upon them. Their history and trials are so doleful, that they have very good reason to wear mourning, and

96

to have a grave-digger's spade on their coat of arms. My own fate, poor knave that I am, is deplorable enough. In one game at cards, I have got the nickname of 'Black Peter!' But alas! I have got a still uglier name, which, indeed, it is hardly the thing to mention aloud," and then he whispered,—"In another game, I have been nicknamed 'Dirty Mads!' I, who was once the King of Spades' Lord Chamberlain! Is not this a bitter fate? The history of my royal master and queen I will not relate; they don't wish me to do so! Little lord of the castle, as he calls himself, may guess it himself if he chooses, but it is very lamentable,—O, no doubt about that! Their circumstances have become very much reduced, and are not likely to change for the better, until we are all riding on the red horse higher than the skies, where there are no haps and mishaps!"

Little William now lighted, as the Knave of Spades had said was proper, three candles for each of the kings, and three for each of the queens; but for the King and Queen of Spades he lighted four candles apiece, and the whole drawing-room became as light and transparent as the palace of the richest emperor, and the illustrious kings and queens bowed to each other serenely and graciously. The Queen of Hearts made her golden fan bow; and the Queen of Spades swung her golden tulip in such a way, that a stream of fire issued from it. The royal couples alighted from the cards and frames, and moved in a slow and graceful minuet up and down the floor. They were dancing in the very midst of flames, and the knaves were dancing too.

But alas! The whole drawing-room was soon in a blaze; the devouring element roared up through the roof, and all was one crackling and hissing sheet of fire; and in a moment little William's castle itself was enveloped in flames and smoke. The boy became frightened, and ran off, crying to his father and mother,—"Fire, fire, fire! my castle is on fire!" He grew pale as ashes, and his little hands trembled like the aspen-leaf. The fire continued sparkling and blazing, but in the midst of this destructive scene, the following words were uttered in a singing tone:—

"Now we are riding on the red horse, higher than the skies! This is the way for kings and queens to go, and this is the way for their knaves to go after them!"

Yes that was the end of William's castle, and of the court cards. William did not perish in the flames; he is still alive, and he washed his small hands, and said: "I am innocent of the destruction of the castle." And, indeed, it was not his fault that the castle was burnt down.

OBÀTÁLÁ

The King of the White Cloth

THE YORÙBÁ people of Southwestern Nigeria have held deep reverence for a group of deities called Orisá, which are considered direct emanations of Olódùmarè, the primordial foundation of all creation. These deities serve as intermediaries through which humans can connect with the divine. One of the most prominent among the Irúnmolè is Obàtálá, known as the King of the White Cloth. Obàtálá represents purity, wisdom and the creative aspects of humanity, offering profound insights into the purpose and motivations of life. Throughout their history, the Yoruba pantheon has encompassed both the constructive and destructive aspects of divinity—it is by embracing both that the Yoruba aspire to a deeper understanding of the divine as well as the natural world that surrounds them.

The creation of mankind

In Yoruba cosmology, Obàtálá (along with Yemoja) is often credited as the creator of humanity. The narrative goes that Olódùmarè tasked Obàtálá with crafting the world. Obàtálá descended from Heaven to Earth using a chain, carrying with him a snail shell filled with sand, a black hen and a palm nut. Upon reaching the water-covered Earth, he spread the sand and released the hen, which began scattering the sand in all directions. Where the sand landed, solid Earth formed, marking the creation of land. Obàtálá called this new place Ilé-Ifẹ—meaning "the land of expansion or dispersion."

With the passing of time, Obàtálá became lonely with only his black hen for company. One day, the great Orisá Yemoja visited. Abundantly pleased with the visit and the chance to have a conversation, Obàtálá related how he was lonely. Because of her love for him, Yemoja decided to stay with Obàtálá, becoming his wife.

When Obàtálá proceeded with the creation of humans, he sculpted them from clays of different densities and colors. After shaping each form, he would call on Olódùmarè to breathe life into them. As the heavenly artisan, Obàtálá sculpted humans in diverse forms, giving rise to a variety of physical features and abilities, fostering the diversity seen among humankind today.

A particularly significant point of the Obàtálá creation story involves his creation of the disabled or differently-abled individuals. According to lore, there was a period when Obàtálá grew fond of palm wine and became intoxicated while creating humans. The sculptures he crafted during this state were imperfect, resulting in physical disabilities. Upon sobering and witnessing the results of his actions, Obàtálá took a vow of sobriety and became the protector of those he had unintentionally disadvantaged, reflecting his caring and remorseful nature. To this day, his worshippers are prohibited from drinking palm wine or using any substance that will greatly alter the state of the mind.

Orişa of calmness

Obàtálá is the Orişá of peace and tranquility and is revered for the calmness of his being and an aura that exudes an unparalleled coolness. With every step, he carries an air of tranquility and poise that captivates all who encounter him. Clad in pristine white garments that symbolize purity and clarity, his wisdom and profound understanding of the world grant him the ability to navigate any situation with grace. Whether mediating conflicts, shaping the destinies of humanity or bringing harmony to the chaotic, Obàtálá's coolness remains unwavering, leaving a lasting impression on those who are fortunate enough to witness his divine presence. He epitomizes the perfect balance between strength and serenity.

Many of Obàtálá's tales recount his extraordinary power as a peacemaker. In one such time it is related that

there was bitter conflict between two neighboring villages. They were locked in an unrelenting battle that threatened to engulf the entire kingdom in bloodshed. The king, who was desperate for a resolution, sought the guidance of Obàtálá. Recognizing the gravity of the situation, Obàtálá set forth on a journey to mediate between the warring villages. With a serene presence and eloquent words, he spoke to the leaders of both sides, reminding them of their shared humanity and the futility of violence. Obàtálá's wisdom and compassion resonated deeply with the warring factions and slowly their hearts softened. Through patient negotiations and a commitment to

A typical offering to Obàtálá is the giant African land snail

understanding, Obàtálá facilitated a peace agreement that brought an end to the conflict. The villagers embraced one another, their weapons replaced by tools of cooperation, and the region flourished under a newfound era of harmony and unity.

In another tale of Obàtálá's remarkable ability to bring peace, a story unfolds recounting a fascinating encounter between two powerful deities, Obàtálá, the deity of creation and wisdom, and Ògún, the deity of iron and warfare. It was a time of great turmoil, as conflicts raged and the dwelling of mankind yearned for peace. Sensing the need for resolution, Obàtálá sought out Ògún, recognizing the importance of his martial prowess and the potential for destruction it carried. Obàtálá sought to bring about peace by appealing to Ògún. Obàtálá

approached Ògún, speaking words of wisdom and appealing to his noble nature. He reminded Ògún of the immense power he possessed and the responsibility that came with it. With their contrasting domains, Obàtálá and Ògún engaged in a profound dialogue, sharing insights and perspectives that transcended their individual roles. Through their interaction, they found common ground and forged a unique partnership. Ògún's strength and determination were tempered by Obàtálá's wisdom and guidance, resulting in a harmonious union that channeled Ògún's might for the greater good of the kingdom. Their alliance brought an era of balance, in which Ògún's energy was channeled towards the protection and prosperity of the people and Obàtálá's wisdom guided their actions. The tale of Obàtálá and

Priests of Obàtálá praying in their shrine.

100

Ògún serves as a testament to the transformative power of collaboration and the potential for harmony even in the most contrasting of forces.

The manifestations of Obàtálá

Many of the Orișá are known to have individual manifestations with separate qualities and attributes representing a distinct aspect of their power and influence. Obàtálá has been known to manifest as a fierce warrior as well as the cool and peaceful ruler. In this manifestation he is the Orișá of courage, wisdom, healing, creativity and justice. Obàtálá has also been known to manifest as a female Orișá. In this emanation Obàtálá is a nurturing, compassionate and mothering being. Through their varied manifestations, the Orișá provide a rich tapestry of virtues and energies that offer guidance, blessings and support to individuals and communities, reminding humans of the vast array of divine qualities that can be tapped into for growth, balance and spiritual connection.

One of Obàtálá's most prominent manifestations is as Obàtálá Aàrẹ the elderly and wise sage. In this form, Obàtálá appears as an aged figure draped in flowing white robes that symbolize purity and wisdom. With a long white beard and a staff in hand, he exudes an aura of profound knowledge and experience. Obàtálá Aàrẹ serves as the embodiment of wisdom, guiding humanity through his sagacious counsel and offering insights into the complexities of life. Through his elderly form, Obàtálá imparts invaluable lessons, reminding humans of the importance of introspection, discernment and making choices that align with higher principles.

Another manifestation of Obàtálá is as Obàtálá Alákètu, the youthful and creative deity. In this form, Obàtálá radiates vitality and virility, appearing as a vibrant and energetic figure whose robe is adorned with intricate patterns and symbols. As Obàtálá Alákètu he inspires creativity, innovation, and artistic expression. He is the patron of craftsmen, artisans and those who seek to bring beauty into the world through their creations. Obàtálá Alákètu embodies the boundless potential within each individual and encourages the exploration of one's talents and passions. Through this manifestation, Obàtálá teaches the importance of embracing one's uniqueness and using it as a catalyst for positive change and self-fulfillment.

The essence of Obàtálá that extends as a female manifestation is known as Obàtálá Ọbàrísanà, a powerful and mothering deity. Obàtálá Ọbàrísanà embodies the feminine qualities of compassion, intuition and fertility. She appears as a regal figure draped in flowing white garments that exude grace and elegance. With a gentle yet resolute demeanor, Obàtálá Ọbàrísanà brings forth the essence of motherhood and nurturing, offering solace, protection and guidance to those in need. As the embodiment of fertility, she is associated with abundance and the cycles of creation. Obàtálá Ọbàrísanà supports and empowers women, advocating for their rights and celebrating their unique contributions to society. Her manifestation serves as a reminder of the sacred feminine energy that flows through the world, nurturing and sustaining life in all its forms.

The shrine of Obàtálá

Those who have gone through *Idosu Obàtálá* (initiation of Obàtálá,) receive the Igba Obàtálá, the calabash or sacred vessel of Obàtálá. At each Orișá initiation the, newly initiated receives a calabash filled with the sacred objects of the Orișá to whom they are initiated. It holds great significance and is considered not only to be sacred, but it is also said to hold the presence of the Orișá to whom the person has been initiated. In the case of the initiate to Obàtálá, the calabash would likely contain a good amount of efun (naturally occurring white chalk) representing the purity of the Orișá, a white cloth indicative of cleanliness, a vessel of clean water which is replaced on a daily basis, a silver bangle, several clean sun-bleached cowries and the divining cowries used for divination at the idosu for the various reading and some objects that are not spoken of publicly. Pointing to his creator of mankind status, his calabash would also have a land snail shell and silver or lead man. The calabash that holds the objects would be painted white with chalk. A white-beaded calabash might house the objects if the initiate could afford as much. Obàtálá has a strong association with elephants, so there might be an object or statue representing an elephant present.

The contents of Igba Obàtálá may vary based on individual practices and personal preferences, but there are some common elements that are typically found within it, such as those enumerated above.

Offerings to Obàtálá

Offerings to Obàtálá typically consist of white or light-colored food and drink, reflecting his association with purity. Among the favorite foods of Obàtálá is pounded yam. Often the pounded yam is formed into little globes that are then piled into a conical shape and offered on a plate that is put on top of the opening to his Igba. Efun is a common offering—often whole pieces are offered. Like all Orișá, a very common offering would be kola nuts. However in the case of Obàtálá, whenever possible he would be offered white kola nuts. Other items that might be offered to him are milk, coconut, white rice and snails. The most important of offerings to Obàtálá is fresh water which must be offered each day. As the Orișá has sworn off alcohol due to the aforementioned myth, it's critical that any offerings made to him are free from alcohol.

Taboos of Obàtálá initiates

The initiates of Obàtálá adhere to certain taboos and restrictions as part of their spiritual practices and dedication to the deity. These taboos are meant to maintain purity, respect and alignment with Obàtálá's energy. While the specific taboos may vary among different lineages and regions, there are some common taboos associated with the priests of Obàtálá. Principal among the taboos is abstention from the use of alcohol and intoxicating substances, in other words the use of anything that clouds the mind. Those who go through initiation to Obàtálá are expected to refrain from wearing red for the first year after initiation, and they would also be told to stay away from bright colors and black. The use of palm oil, while not prohibited, is discouraged, and shea butter might be used for cooking instead.

Among the most important of taboos is the avoidance of negative speech and action. Priests are expected to maintain a respectful and harmonious demeanor, refraining from engaging in gossip, slander or any form of negative speech or action that may disrupt balance and purity.

It is important to note that taboos and restrictions can vary and individual priests may have additional personal commitments or obligations specific to their initiation and lineage. The purpose of these taboos is to create a sacred space for the devotee to connect deeply with Obàtálá's energy and to honor the deity through their actions, thoughts and behaviors.

Rituals and offerings for Obàtálá

Rituals for Obàtálá aim to invoke his blessings, guidance and protection. The ceremonies often involve chants, prayers and music, with the kettle drum as well as the bata drum playing sacred rhythms that range from slow and stately to ebullient tones. While the dances of many other Oriṣá may be frenetic, those of Obàtálá are regal and can be joyous without being overpowering. The lyrical content of the songs and chants usually includes praises, supplications and recounting of his myths and deeds.

Obàtálá's narrative is more than just a tale of creation—it carries enduring wisdom and lessons of morality, compassion and tolerance. By embodying purity and peace, he teaches us the importance of leading a life of truth and tranquility. His role as a divine artist urges his worshippers to appreciate diversity and respect all forms of human existence. His remorse

Candomble statue of Obàtálá

for his actions during his drunken state serves as a reminder of the detrimental consequences of intoxication and a call for responsibility in personal actions.

In our increasingly diverse and complex world, Obàtálá's principles are relevant and needed more than ever. By understanding and imbibing the lessons from his narrative, we can aspire to create a society that values peace, purity and respect for diversity—attributes that define the revered Oriṣá, Obàtálá.

—IFADOYIN SANGOMUYIWA

103

Bàtà-banta nínú àlà

Ósùn nínú àlà

Ó jí nínú àlà

Ó ti inú àlà dìde

Immense in white robe,

He sleeps in white clothes,

He wakes up in white clothes,

He rises in white clothes.

–traditional praise poetry for Obàtálá

How to Create a Shakespeare Garden

A SHAKESPEARE garden is a garden that references items in Shakespeare's works. You can create a garden based on any writer's works but Shakespeare gives the reader a bit more to work with than others. In contrast, in J.R.R. Tolkien's works—and in particular in his elf-kingdom of Lothlorien—his flora is entirely fictional! As a friend once said, "there are no Mallorn trees here." Similarly, Kingsfoil—a plant famously used for healing in Tolkien's work—is mere fiction. But the Bard names plants that actually exist in the real world and these can be a point of reference for creating a themed garden. It is easy to picture an old Victorian-style manor house with a run-down Shakespeare garden, perfect for lingering ghosts!

To create your garden, carefully consider your resources. For example, there are sites such as

www.botanicalshakespeare.com but be cautious—words do not all mean the same things that they used to. A reference to "lime" on the above site, for example, does not mean a small green fruit but an amount of a sticky lime substance used to catch birds. When selecting plants, you should also look not just at the words themselves but at how they were used in the context of an older version of the English language and the symbolism they carried. For example, in *Hamlet* Ophelia in her madness talks about herbs and their meanings:

There's rosemary, that's for remembrance. Pray you, love, remember. And there is pansies, that's for thoughts ...

There's fennel for you, and columbines. There's rue for you, and here's some for me; we may call it herb-of-grace o'

105

Sundays. You must wear your rue with a difference. There's a daisy. I would give you some violets, but they withered all when my father died. They say he made a good end

-Act IV, Scene V, Hamlet
William Shakespeare

This one passage includes rosemary, fennel and rue. Anyone who's cooked with herbs ought to recognize rosemary and fennel. Rue is more obscure for Americans but is a strongly scented, bitter European perennial. Planting according to this passage would yield a garden that's half filled with herbs, half filled with flowers and full of symbolism.

Knowing the language of flower symbolism makes Ophelia's words all that much more poignant. Daisies are attributed with hope and new beginnings. Columbines are hardy flowers that grow in diverse conditions and so they are symbols of endurance and perseverance. Violets have a variety of meanings: innocence, everlasting love, modesty, spiritual wisdom, faithfulness, mysticism and remembrance.

Because of their long association with love, Shakespeare mentions roses in *Romeo and Juliet* and in so many of his sonnets. Juliet ponders the silly fact that a mere name should keep her from her Romeo when she says, "What's in a name? That which we call a rose, by any other name would smell as sweet." Any kind of rose can be added to a Shakespeare garden but should you be able to find it, there is actually a variety of rose that has been dubbed the "William Shakespeare rose." This rose has a deep, blushing pink color and an abundance of petals.

If you do choose to add roses, there is another way to incorporate them into a Shakespeare garden—you could set aside a section of the garden for red and white roses as a nod to the historical Wars of the Roses waged for the throne of England. The houses of Lancaster and York fought a series of civil wars that lasted from 1455 to 1485. Be sure to label the red roses with a "Lancaster" marker and the white roses with a "York" marker.

Consider also how you will use the edible plants you include in food and other applications. Mint, for example, is delicious when you add a few fresh leaves to a cup of tea. There are few things in this world that are more refreshing! Shakespeare mentions mint in *The Winter's Tale*: "Here's flowers for you; hot lavender, mints, savory, marjoram." He calls these—along with marigolds—herbs for middle-aged men! Lavender is easy to grow in a garden and is delightfully fragrant. It can be added to tea and other hot drinks for a calming influence. The

buds of the lavender flower can be picked and added to a sleep pouch to release their fragrance while you sleep. All of the herbs in the passage above are included in traditional Herbes de Provence blends. Simply add them to thyme and oregano and use the mixture to add a subtle complexity to meat, fish and soups, or dust on cheeses and over oil.

Now there are things to add to a garden and things not to add. Although the Witches of Macbeth add "root of hemlock, digged i' the dark" to their potion, it's poisonous and invasive and you'll end up having to pull it up frequently as it spreads wildly. Tradition holds that Socrates was made to die by drinking hemlock—it's nasty stuff.

Hemlock is not the only invasive Shakesperean plant—many herbs tend to take over whatever they are planted in, but most especially mint and rosemary. One trick to minimize spread is to put pots in the ground in order to grow herbs but have them somewhat contained. Examples of this type of herb gardening can be found on Pinterest.

All the plants discussed above are easy to find and to grow—start with these to put together a basic Shakespeare garden. When you are ready to add more plants, spend a few evenings looking through the Bard's works to see what flora is mentioned and then check if it's available in your local area or if seeds or small plants can be shipped to your area. When you are ordering seeds, be aware that most flowers are annuals and need to be replanted every year. Add statues, signs and markers with quotes from the plays and…voila! You are ready to enjoy your Shakespeare garden.

—MARINA BRYONY

Lake Huron's White Rock

The Sacred Cornerstone of Michigan's Thumb

MICHIGAN HIGHWAY 25 is a scenic two-lane road which traces the shoreline of Lake Huron on Michigan's Thumb. It is an area rich in history and mystical traditions. About ten miles South of Harbor Beach and just North of Forester is a beautiful lakefront park with a historic marker. The marker commemorates White Rock, a sacred Native American site specific to the indigenous people known as the Anishinaabe.

Today tourists often find flowers, coins, fruits and other tokens left near the marker stone and plaque which tells the legend of White Rock. A path winds away from the marker and parking lot through a stretch of forest leading to an overlook on the Great Lake. Following this pathway, an otherworldly atmosphere builds. It is a place heavy with a sacred silence and the fragrance of evergreens. Gazing across the water about a half mile offshore, a bright white rock is visible. The vibes deepen. There is definitely the sense of being in a sacred place.

At present the White Rock is about twelve feet across. Two or three hundred years ago it was very much larger. Since then, rising water levels have carved away and covered much of the original limestone boulder. During World War II the United States military used the rock

108

for target practice, dropping bombs which contributed to its now diminished size. Yet the bright White Rock in the Great Lake is unmistakable—it stands out. It still suggests, to those who are sensitive to such energies, the presence of Great Manitou—the Great Spirit venerated by the Anishinaabe.

The White Rock was used as a boundary and navigation marker for centuries. The Anishinaabe were grateful for the unusual bounty of the Thumb region. Offerings of tobacco, herbs, fish and game as well as sacred items were left on White Rock as gifts of appreciation for the riches given to them by Great Manitou. Ceremonies and rituals were conducted on it to honor and draw the favors of the Great Spirit. During the nineteenth century settlers built a thriving town nearby called White Rock. There were hotels, a school, dance hall, church and a variety of thriving businesses. In 1860 a group of the townspeople decided to have a square dance on the White Rock. The

remaining Native Americans warned them not to do this, but the party crowd ignored the advice. They traveled in canoes for the event. One man felt uneasy and decided to remain floating in his canoe instead of landing on the Rock. He ended up witnessing the two lightning bolts. These simultaneously struck The Rock and killed every one of the square dancers.

In October of 1875 a great fire swept across the region. The town of White Rock was completely destroyed. Today there is only a tiny unincorporated village near the site. Some attribute these events to the wrath of Manitou. Who can say?

White Rock Park is free to visit. It is a memorable stop for meditation and reflection. More information is available on the website https://www. michigan.org/city/white-rock. There are also Youtube videos and podcasts which elaborate on the odd history of White Rock.

—ESTHER NEUMEIER

Log On

Surfing The Wood Wide Web

AT A GLANCE a group of trees can seem solitary, even lonely. They can give an impression of being self contained individuals standing apart and aloof. Yet legends of talking, socially aware and sacred trees belie this. There have long been hints that the consciousness of trees is expansive and extensive. Researchers and scientists from around the world working in more than 70 different countries—including the United States, Canada, the United Kingdom and Switzerland—have compiled a data base called The Global Forest initiative. The gist of this project is recognizing and exploring how a subterranean world

of roots and fungi—teeming with life—exists beneath our feet. It's a complicated web woven of bacteria, tiny mushrooms (fungi) and roots. Its purpose is to allow trees to communicate with and help each other. Coined the Wood Wide Web, it is actually the oldest and largest of all social networks. The interconnectedness of trees—The Wood Wide Web—predates the internet and humanity itself by as much as 450 million years!

Studies show that trees speak their own language—they share information about insects, warning each other to produce bitter compounds to protect against destructive pests. Dying trees share their DNA with seedlings to help them grow. Through photosynthesis trees produce much more glucose than they need for themselves in order to transmit it to nourish seedlings. Some trees such as the black walnut are antisocial, though. They will attack other trees by producing toxins. Within an established forest are large, older hubs or mother trees. They are the dominant, or secret leaders of this underground world. Studies have shown that one hub tree can network with as many as forty-seven other trees!

Dr. Susanne Simard, a professor of forestry at The University of British Columbia, has written a book, *Finding the Mother Tree*, about this social network, the conscious world of the forest. The trees have a fascinating social awareness. They cooperate, socialize and share information related to their health and vulnerable points. Findings indicate that trees have communities which are not all that different from our own neighborhoods. Thin white strands of mushroom like organisms called mycorrhizal fungi are at the core of this Wood Wide Web. Neither plants nor animals, but something in between, these mushroom-like organisms aid trees in transmitting and sharing vital nutrients and information. A careful study of tree roots will find them wrapped in colorful fungi in shades of yellow, purple, white and more. These form an intertwining carpet beneath the ground which is actually the link system in this separate world of the trees. The fungi emerge as mushrooms appearing above ground, often after a rainfall. Without roots or seeds, they are just present. They are valuable to Earth's life cycles. Like reincarnation, they bring new life from decay. This magical world of fungi has been credited with providing mushrooms which offer significant health benefits and gourmet delicacies. The mushrooms have long inspired superstitions, folklore, myths and references to sacred magical powers.

Over a century ago Beatrix Potter, the beloved Victorian writer and illustrator most often remembered for her children's stories of Peter Rabbit and other characters such as Squirrel Nutkin and Benjamin Bunny, actually began to study what is now called the Wood Wide Web. She created detailed paintings of mushrooms. She even won early acclaim as a mycologist until being expelled from academic circles because of her gender. Eventually Potter used the fortune she earned through publishing to become involved in the conservation of England's Lake District. Preserving the ancient forests from development and donating lands and original manuscripts to England's National Trust to benefit future generations, Beatrix Potter was an early ecologist and preservationist. She left hints that reveal how she might have been the first to recognize the importance of the interconnectedness of trees long before the arrival of the Wood Wide Web and Global Forest initiative of today!

—DIKKI-JO MULLEN

111

22 Shades of Gray

THE NEXT MOST important book to be written about the Western Magical Tradition for the 21st Century should be about the Hermetic Order of the Golden Dawn and its extraordinary system. I would suggest that the title and the theme be simply *They Got a Few Things Wrong.*

The problem has been that we're all in thrall to the intellectual genius of McGregor Mathers and in awe of the visionary talents of his wife Moina. We tend to see them as rarefied beings, austere exemplars of the Magical Arts who are closer to the Gods than us mortals. We tend to project onto them a kind of papal infallibility and rarely have the nerve to challenge what they created.

If we could 'remote view' the Mathers when they were creating

their system we would see young Moina, fresh from art college and doing nothing worthwhile with her talent that her parents would approve of, seemingly in the shadow of the jobless and apparently unemployable man who wanted everyone to call him McGregor. Don't see them as grey-haired ancients: see one very absorbed and very young woman working at the behest of her slightly older uber-intense partner. Admire their passion and excitement as you watch them bringing through their teachings by means of the intense psychism we expect of them, augmented by techniques as surprising and unreliable as the dowsing pendulum to give them a straight Yes or No from the Mighty Ones, and—also surprisingly—the Ouija Board. Admire, but don't be in awe. They were, comparatively, mere youngsters when they did all this.

They did their work—or rather their Work—in grotty rooms, with never enough to eat, never enough light in the evenings, and no clear certainty that they would ever get any material profit from their efforts. They were almost like a couple today from the Benefit Culture except theirs came, eventually, not from the state but from the largesse of Annie Horniman, who was one of their first neophytes and most loyal supporter.

I'm not being denigratory here. Mathers was *the* great magus of the past 150 years. No-one else has come close. And as far I personally am concerned, I fell in love with Moina when I first saw that photograph of her at the Slade College of Art and nothing has changed since.

But they were very human, and very fallible when it came to putting together their system. Some of the rituals, like the Lesser Banishing Ritual of the Pentagram, are like steam engines which generate enormous power and proceed with a kind of majestic but clunking beauty throwing out sparks, steam, and a lot of wasted energy.

I think it was the kabbalist James Sturzaker who argued that Moina got 75% of the Colour Scales on the Tree of Life wrong, but because she got them right at Briah-tic levels, they still worked. In a number of cases their apparently inspired system of Correspondences just do not correspond. They get results, as we all know and have experienced, but sometimes it's a case of fitting square pegs into round holes. Which actually can be done, and quite easily, if you've got a big enough hammer and bash the pegs until the corners splinter.

And in some ways they were cursed by the felicity of the number 22.

The 22 paths on the Tree of Life, 22 letters in the Hebrew alphabet (this is not a spelling error), and 22 cards in the Major Arcana of the tarot were crying out for a neat and obvious fit. The initial match was done simply by putting the first tarot card on the first path and matching it with the first Hebrew letter—which was also a number. (I have to confess that I don't even know what letter/number this is, because I've deliberately never learned Hebrew, and reject the notion that it is a 'sacred language' when the letters are demonstrably simplified version of much older Egyptian hieroglyphs.)

A few magicians such as Crowley, Frater Achad and Paul Foster Case determined their own systems of tarot/Tree correspondences, but they never ventured far from the original, and were all still hooked onto the Hebrew letters. It was an outwardly tough but inwardly warm Englishwoman called Bobbie Gray who, in the mid-60s, said to her husband: "Why does it have to be in bloody Hebrew? What's that got to do with us here?" Her husband Bill, too old to be an *enfant terrible* but most definitely something of an *eminence grise* by this time, looked at the whole Golden Dawn system and agreed. Working at remarkable speed and with serendipity of funding, he

Left Hand Pillar	Middle Pillar	Right Hand Pillar
Hermit		Hierophant
Death	Star	Emperor
Hanged Man		Temperance
Devil		Empress
Blasted Tower	Sun	Strength
Chariot		Lovers
Magus	Moon	High Priestess
Fool		World

wrote a little known book which turned Mathers' system on its head.

William G. Gray's *Magical Ritual Methods* is a work of pure genius. Just one chapter alone, on ritual sonics, is still light years ahead of anything that is being done today. His version of the Banishing Ritual, for example, is superbly elegant and wonderfully simple, using a ring-pass-not kind of structure which utilises the concepts of Time Space and Event, and four (English) vowel-sounds. The whole book has been plundered, stolen from and used without acknowledgement so often that today, two generations later, there is a whole breed of young magicians, witches, kabbalists, Rosicrucians and druids who imagine that their techniques derive from the ancient temples of Greece, Rome and Egypt—or else from the dark, primordial glades of the Wildwood. But they don't: they came from 14 Bennington Street in Cheltenham.

Gray didn't take sole credit for his sublime system of tarot correspondences. He told me quite

candidly that these came directly from his inner contact with the spirit of Dion Fortune. Likewise, when he detailed these correspondences in the large and later tome *The Talking Tree*, Bobbie told me that when she was taking down his dictation she often couldn't tell whether it was Bill speaking to her or Dion. I make no judgement on this, I simply pass on what was said.

Bill (or was it the spirit of DF?) showed that the Waite/Rider Tarot had an inherent system of cohesion that didn't need anyone to bash their square pegs into round holes as they developed their magic. He ignored the numbering of the cards and instead went for their sense, matching the positive cards with the right-hand pillar, the negative cards with the left, and putting the Moon/Sun/Star on the Middle Pillar. He described the right-hand pillar as being concerned with what he termed, anabolic' or building-up energies, while the left-hand pillar expressed the, katabolic' or breaking-down processes. And the cards reflected this.

114

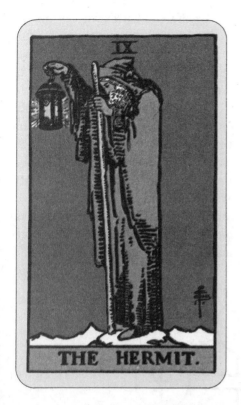

THE HERMIT.

THE EMPRESS.

Much of this is encapsulated in the table on the previous page.

They are conjoined by Judgement, Justice and the Wheel of Fortune, which Gray defined as Fatal or Karmic on three distinct levels of compensatory energy.

But there is also a cohesive integrity between the cards from top to bottom, as well as right and left: The Fool and World might be thought of as un-initiated, inexperienced humanity: the know-all, and the person who is wrapped up in himself. Above them are the High Priestess and the Magician, balancing each other in the appropriate way. While at the very top of the Tree are the Hierophant and the Hermit, teaching humanity by precept and example respectively.

Look at the Hermit from the Waite pack: if his staff represents the Middle Pillar, the lamp is at the place of Binah. What is the Magical Image of Kether? —an ancient bearded king seen in profile. What are the colours of Binah? Why is he standing on a mountain-top? Really—and just forget those damned Hebrew letters for once—where else could the Hermit go but on the path between Binah and Kether?

Connecting Binah with Tiphereth is the Hanged Man. His head is radiant (in the Sun), his legs are crossed to form the astrological symbol for Saturn, which is the, mundane chakra' as they used to say, for Binah.

And then there is The Empress, connecting Chesed whose Magical Image involves regality and a throne, with Netzach, whose Magical Image invokes a beautiful naked woman. There is even a heart-shaped shield next to her throne which bears the glyph of Venus, the planet of Netzach. All right, The Empress isn't naked, but look at the beautiful naked female figure of The World which connects Netzach with Malkuth.

Every card in the Waite pack, using this system of correspondences as determined by William Gray and inspired by Dion Fortune, comes alive when put in these contexts. Those readers who were in a sense 'brought up' by the Golden Dawn system and wedged tightly into it, might find the whole thing disturbing. But look through, and give it a go, and be prepared to be astonished.

However, if the title of the next book on Mathers' system should be *They Got a Few Things Wrong*, it should also have the subtitle *But They Did Their Best*. And they did it magnificently. Which is no more or less than we all must do in this business of magic, no matter how primitive our early efforts might seem.

—ALAN RICHARDSON

Wm. G. Gray's tarot correspondences.

116

Traditional British Smudging : Juniper Smoke

SAGE smudging exploded into popular Wiccan practice in the 2000s in North America. It is a borrowing from the First Nations peoples of the western Plains, for whom white sage is a sacred plant. It once grew abundantly there and in many indigenous cultures, people use it to purify the energies of a space. In ceremony this is done in particular ways with particular tools. Wiccan spellcraft draws heavily from the magics of many populations in the U.S. and Canada and this has included sage smudging.

British people and folk across Europe have used smoke purifying for hundreds of years. In the European landscape the plant for smoking and smudging was not

sage, however. Rather it was the sacred and powerful juniper plant. Many people knew the juniper as savin, or saffern or even saffron and everyone knew it had the power to repel negative forces, which used to be framed as "evil spirits." One old book says, "Juniper is regarded with great veneration," because, "it has the power and privilege of putting to flight the spirits of evil and destroying the charms of the evil magicians." Sage simply wasn't used.

When European immigrants crossed the Atlantic to start their new lives in America, they left behind their juniper magic. Knowledge of juniper's power stayed in the Old Country, so today's Witches and Pagans in the USA and

117

Canada don't have it in their repertoire. However, as the passion for "smudging" is at a peak, it's a perfect time to revive juniper smoke magic. If you adopt it in place of sage smudging, it protects the dwindling white sage crops and it shows respect for your Native neighbours.

Juniper smoke protection was almost universal across Scotland and Wales and across much of England until a hundred years ago. Everyone knew about it and everyone did it. Nor was it just on the British Isles—documents indicate that it was a common practice in other parts of Europe, too. Housewives, workmen, blacksmiths and cattlemen would regularly go outside into their backyards, pick juniper branches, dry them at home, then stick them into their open fires to set them alight and get the smoke going. A few do it still. They break off twigs from the juniper tree and then dry them and bundle them with string. When it is time to purify a space, they light the bundle with a lighter then waft it around the house or workplace. People who have larger spaces like barns will dry entire juniper branches, then light them to create a torch of billowing, smoldering protective smoke that they carry. It's as easy as making a sage bundle.

The juniper tree is a highly aromatic evergreen that has potent purple-black berries. It grows all over Europe—by roadsides, in scrubland and in gardens. It is incredibly common! The green needles smell a bit like pine—cleansing and sharp but with a distinct edge that is unique, almost fruity and dark.

The sap of the juniper tree is plentiful, sticky and almost oily so the wood of the twigs and branches gives off a heady scent even when one first picks it. For this reason, it's no surprise that juniper doesn't even need to be burnt to be effective in magical protection. Branches simply picked and brought indoors will work, too! Records of hundreds of old European customs demonstrate this. For example, to keep out evil, the folklorists of England say that "boughs of juniper are suspended before the doorways." Italians used to pick a branch, bring it into the house and sweep across the home's openings to keep out evil spirits. Norwegians and Swedes used to strew branches of juniper on their wooden floors. In one part of Germany, when babies were unwell, the local good Witch would put out a tray with a sprig of juniper, a bunch of wool, and a piece bread on it—these items would distract

118

the spirit of the sickness who would forget the baby and go to eat the piece of bread, spin the wool and count the many tiny juniper needles. The baby was then free to recover.

The berries of the juniper are sacred and powerful, too. In some regions, people used to pick the berries, dry them, then put them onto coals to smoulder. The ancient Greeks and Romans knew the juniper as being sacred to the Furies so they burned berries this way at funerals, too, believing the smoke kept away demons. In the later Christian centuries, farming areas couldn't access Catholic-favored resins like frankincense, so juniper was the homegrown equivalent of demon-banishing incense. To this day, some more traditional Witches in the UK and Europe are taught to use juniper berries for protection: burnt on charcoals, strung on a thread or even infused in alcohol and drunk—that's good old fashioned gin! Gin is an alcohol which is always flavored with juniper, which is the ingredient which gives it its distinctive flavor. It is a Witchy fact that gin-making started out as medical-magical potion process.

We hope that Witches will embrace juniper smoke as a replacement for sage smudging. It's easy, ecological and respectful to the Native nations. But if drying and burning is too much, the modern Witch can connect with the juniper spirit in an even easier way—by drinking a glass of gin. Spirit Juniper will infuse itself through your body and bless and protect you. We can all raise a glass to that.

−CHRISTINA OAKLEY HARRINGTON

Christina Oakley Harrington is the founder and proprietor of Treadwell's Bookshop in London. A practitioner of British Witchcraft, she is also author of The Treadwell's Book of Plant Magic. *To read the Witches' Almanc review of this important book go to https://thewitchesalmanac.com/pages/the-treadwells-book-of-plant-magic*

LUPERCALIA
Reenactment, revelry and purification

In the days before Rome in the region of Latium in central Italy, the story goes that Numitor—a descendant of Venus herself through the Trojan hero Aeneas—ruled the city of Alba Longa. He was a just and wise king, but his wicked brother Amulius usurped Numitor's throne, killing all of Numitor's sons. Amulius allowed his niece Rhea Silvia to live but forced her into chastity by consecrating her to the maiden Goddess Vesta. Unable to resist her great beauty and unwilling to let such injustice go unchecked, the God Mars slept with her in secret and when her pregnancy became known, Amulius locked Rhea Silvia away. Eventually her twin sons Romulus and Remus were born and the king ordered a servant to kill the babes. Not having the heart to carry out this order directly, the servant threw the basket with the twin boys into the flooded Tiber. There the river God Tibernus calmed his waters and guided the basket to catch in the roots of a fig tree that dangled down into the water at the base of the Palatine A mother wolf happened by and began to suckle the babes, keeping them alive until they were discovered by Amulius' shepherd,

Faustulus. The kind herder and his wife raised the children as shepherds. They disclosed to the boys their true identity when they became young men and the noble twins killed the fiend Amulius and restored Numitor to his throne. Like their ancestor Aeneas, Romulus and Remus were pious and would not unseat their grandfather from his place, but unwilling to wait for their inheritance, the twins set out to found a city of their own.

They had a disagreement about the site for their city—Remus favored the Aventine Hill while Romulus preferred the Palatine, the very area near the Tiber where the good shepherd Faustulus had found them. Romulus and Remus began to argue and looked to the sky for a sign of whose part the Gods would take. The omens were unclear, though, with Remus seeing six birds first and Romulus seeing twelve. Romulus began to build the wall of his city despite the disagreement, but Remus was still bitter from the quarrel and he jumped over the low barrier to make fun of it. Romulus struck him

over the head with his spade, killing him, and declared that the same fate would meet any who dared to breach the walls of Rome.

The cave where the wolf suckled the twins was called the *Lupercal* and was a sacred site in historical times. There the Luperci priests of Faunus celebrated the festival of Lupercalia for over a thousand years. On February 15th, the Romans gathered at the Lupercal where the Luperci—a name meaning "wolf-men"—offered cakes and sacrificed a dog and goats. Then two patrician boys of noble blood would step forward. The Luperci touched the boys' foreheads with the bloody knives, and then others wiped off the blood with scraps of wool soaked in milk and the boys laughed. Perhaps in doing this, the boys became Romulus and Remus, the noble twins who were sentenced to death but saved by the nourishment of the wolf. Afterwards, they cut the skins of the sacrificed goats into strips called *februa* and ran naked through the city. Wearing only februa strips as belts, they struck anyone in their paths with the

februa. This circuit of the city reenacted the celebratory race of the companions of Romulus and Remus who sprinted to the Lupercal in celebration once they had defeated Amulius. Purification by the februa was thought to help a woman conceive and so those hoping for a child would throw themselves in the path of the Luperci.

By starting at the Lupercal, these ceremonies were deeply tied to the founding myths of Rome and maintaining the festival remained an important obligation of the state throughout Rome's history. Enacting the festival annually ensured the safety and prosperity of Rome. There was a great deal of revelry and the festival was so popular that in Christian times, the church had difficulty putting a stop to it. At the end of the fifth century, Pope Gelasius I finally settled on transforming the ancient purification festival on the 15th of February into a feast of the purification of the Virgin Mary, which was moved to February 2nd and renamed Candlemas, and the race around the city was replaced with a procession of candles. He faced resistance from the Roman nobility, though, who were by that time all Christian. They argued that foregoing the Lupercalia festival would bring calamities to the city—plagues, failed harvests and wars—and that the Byzantines in the East would overtake them in wealth and prominence, which, of course, they did.

—MAB BORDEN

Two youths of noble birth run,

smiting all those whom they meet,

as once with brandished weapons,

down from Alba's heights,

Remus and Romulus ran.

—*Plutarch's* Life of Romulus,
tr. Bernadotte Perrin, 1914

122

Merry Meetings

*A candle in the window, a fire on the hearth,
a discourse over tea…*

AS TREADWELLS in London is in its twentieth year, Christina Oakley Harrington is continually busy creating a very unique space for the esoteric literati and magical communities. Prior to publicly being known as a occultist, Christina pursued an academic track earning a PhD in medieval history as well as privately studying esoteric traditions. Her recent ground breaking books—*The Treadwell's Book of Plant Magic* and *Dreams of Witches*—have quickly become volumes of note in both the Wiccan and Pagan communities.

How and when did Treadwells come into being? What was the initial inspiration for you?

Treadwells in London opened its doors twenty years ago, on May Day 2003. I founded it because I believe passionately in bookshops as places where people and ideas can come together. So much of the 1890s Golden Dawn cultural flowering happened in London because people met one another at Watkins Bookshop, for example. In Paris in the early 20th century, a great deal of the LGBTQ literary scene centred around Sylvia Beach's bookshop Shakespeare & Co. So the bookshop as a cultural hub, a salon, appealed to me. I was flattered and taken aback to read that Treadwell's is now considered to most famous occult bookshop in the world. I feel, the more the merrier, but if we are well known, it suggests we're doing something right. We welcome everyone in a friendly way—old, young, gay, straight, magical, muggle, rich, poor. Inclusiveness is baked into our vision.

How have you seen the occult scene of London change over the years and what do you see for the future?

London's occult scene has changed quite a bit. In the early to mid-twentieth century, everyone was joining magical orders and Covens. In the 1980s and 1990s a huge social-magical scene flowered which was centred upon fortnightly Pub Moots—gatherings in the rooms of pubs, with speakers, networking, socialising and matchmaking. The most famous was Talking Stick, which ran for a couple decades, and every second Tuesday night some fifty or sixty magical people of all stripes convened to a central London establishment to eat, drink, listen to an expert talk, and socialise. There absolutely was a scene! It has died away, and nowadays people make personal and magical connections online and meet more privately. The continuity since the 1800s, however, is the esoteric bookshops. It's still normal to meet a friend at the occult bookshop and, striking up a conversation, to make new friends.

For the future, I'm really curious! As London has become more expensive, younger folk are living in East London and now further out in Southeast and Northeast London—it means our central location in Bloomsbury is not a short distance from people's homes any more, unlike twenty years ago. However, we are around the corner from the British Museum, so we are handy for anyone who might be going there to visit the many Goddess statues and ancient religious icons. As the internet becomes more and more flooded, too, we find folk seeking us out in person to get guidance on what is genuinely good to read! Also our booksellers answer a lot of questions: people get bombarded online with mountains of contradictory informa-tion, so we are here as longterm practitioners to help with knowledge.

What are the must-see sites in London if you're magically inclined?

If you're magically-inclined, you must go the British Museum, the home of the statues and objects of the world's pagan religions, ancient and recent. In two hours you can meet Isis, Sekhmet, Pachamama, Aphrodite, Avalokitishwara, Oshun, Ishtar, Inanna, Pan, Dionysos, Ogun, Set, Osiris and other deities whose names are lost but whose images are before you, crafted by their worshippers. There are ritual objects galore, from everywhere—including the scrying and angel-summoning tablets and

124

THE TREADWELL'S BOOK OF

PLANT MAGIC

CHRISTINA OAKLEY HARRINGTON

crystals of the Elizabethan astrologer-angel-occultist John Dee. Everyone who is pagan should visit the River Thames, which runs right through the city. For thousands of years, we have been making offerings into her waters, dropping our magical talismans off the bridges into the flowing currents and—in Celtic times—worshipping her as our local Goddess.

Where did folks go for books in the early days of Wicca (pre internet!)?

Before the internet, the bookshop was the place to go for Witchcraft books, ceremonial magic books—all of it. The bookseller, there in the store, was your guide, your curator, your Goodreads! The bookshops also used to have notice boards and Covens, magical lodges and Druid groups would pin a little card to the cork board. Many, if not most, people found their way into organised

groups through those little pinned slips of card—they would copy down the phone number or the postal address onto the back of an envelope, then go home and either phone from the landline or get out their stationery and handwrite a short letter introducing themselves—to strangers. It wasn't for the faint-hearted.

Treadwell's has come to be a hub for and impacted the occult and Pagan community over the years. How is that changing your approach to the needs of the community?

Since Day One, we have had a commitment to being a safe space. The UK occult scene, like any subculture, always has a few predatory men who hover around, ready to flatter the young seeker, and to groom them into a compromising relationship. Usually they are great name-droppers, and always extremely charming

and—on the surface—gentlemanly. Less common, but still real, are abusive Coven leaders. So our staff, our classes, our parties, make a place where those people are not present, where we make referrals to places that we know to be wholesome and we answer any and all questions that newer folk might have about their experiences in the wider magical community. I myself love books and spent so much of my youth in bookshops, that for me, the bookshop is a kind of temple.

Tell us a little bit about your journey into the Occult.

I trained as an academic for my day job—my undergraduate degree was at an Ivy League College and my Masters and PhD were at University of London, supplemented by tutorials at Oxford. Then I was a professor for eleven years. I've always written and researched, and in recent years I get to do more of that. But that's the outer world. In my personal life, I got involved in Paganism, then Wicca, in the 1980s, and since then I've been active both in a private spiritual/magical way, and also involved in the wider Pagan community. I served as an officer of the Pagan Federation in the 1990s and since 2003 have been active in the UK Pagan community through Treadwell's, which is face-to-face, in person, which suits me best. I'd maybe sum things up by saying that my spiritual life is pretty private, centred upon my relationship

126

with the sacred—but my Pagan community life focusses on being a force for good in the world to the best of my ability.

In Dreams of the Witches you explore some material from the early days of Wicca and the New Forest Coven and Gerald Gardner. Can you tell us a bit about this?

My current research has me diving into the early history of the religio-pagan Witchcraft revival around the New Forest area in the 1920s and 1930s. It was this small but pre-existing movement of about 20 people that Gerald Gardner joined in the late 1930s. Archival research of recent years demonstrates Gardner didn't make it all up after all. The findings are presented in Philip Heselton's books In Search of the New Forest Coven *and* Witchfather.

The New Forest friends formed an ecstatic practice to be shared with a few close friends, in which people would experience joyful free dancing, trance possession, drumming, song and words of

beauty and power under a Full Moon. The small network of suffragette bohemians were forward looking as they revived a life-affirming Paganism, working from what they liked about mystery religions in ancient Greece—in a free, shamanic way. To them, friendship mattered more than polarity did. My recent book Dreams of Witches *shares some of the poetry, vision and lightness that made up the world of those Witches. The early Craft in the UK, which came to be called 'Gardnerian' was freer, more feminist and fun than anyone can imagine. We now know that two of the earliest covens had a (welcomed and treasured) trans priestess in their direct lineage. And that Patricia and Arnold Crowther, and Doreen Valiente, going way back to the 1960s, were vocal in their inclusion of LGBT folk. So there are quite a few misconceptions about "the early days" we're finding. It is very revealing and surprising and makes me mindful that we can often under estimate our forbears.*

127

ASTROLOGY OF THE
NATIONAL GEOGRAPHIC SOCIETY
How To Read Horoscopes for Corporations

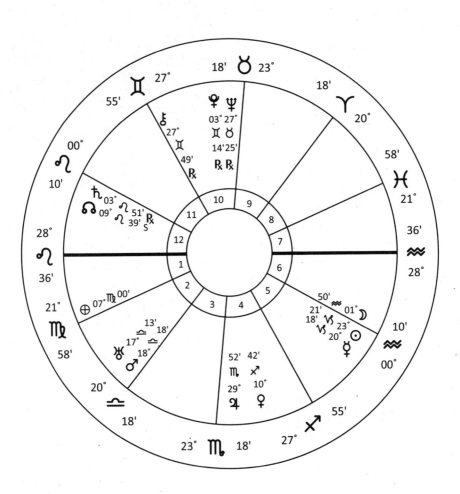

Mundane astrology refers to the special horoscopes cast for businesses and organizations and …it's anything but boringly mundane! Rather, this type of astrology is thrilling and so useful as a tool in seeking truly meaningful messages written in the stars.

Astrology touches each and every part of daily life. Large and small, natural or man made, everything has a beginning for which its own birth chart can be prepared. Predictable events are shown in the chart just as predictions are made for a person's life. Companies also employ astrologers in connection with human resources, checking on the birth data of job candidates, to ascertain which would be the best fit with the company. The purchase of a new refrigerator, automobile, race horse or anything at all can be helped along by using astrology. Publisher's Weekly once compared *National Geographic* to "motherhood, apple pie and the American flag." Few institutions have touched the lives of so many of us for such a long period of time. As a study in mundane astrology, the "thing" that is *National Geographic*'s longevity suggested that its astrology chart must show some celestial indicators of long life and power. Generations and generations of people find joy in its pages of colorful photographs and stories about exotic animals, far away places and, what it is mostly about, unfamiliar people.

When did National Geographic begin? That will reveal its horoscope.

The *National Geographic* Society, which publishes the magazine, is a Capricorn. It began over a century ago at 8:00 pm on Friday, January 13, 1888, in Washington, DC. The unique magic of Friday (the weekday ruled by Venus) added to the legendary serendipity of Friday the 13th was certainly at work. It was a Venus planetary hour too. Something really wonderful was born. It was an exclusive group of thirty-three distinguished gentlemen who gathered near the White House and formed a club. Inventors, teachers, bankers, as well as military officers and naturalists all affirmed that they wanted to form a society to increase and diffuse geographic knowledge

about the world, its lands, its history and its people. They were to succeed beyond their wildest dreams.

Today the National Geographic Society has assets of hundreds of millions of dollars. In 1984 President Reagan spoke at the dedication of the Society's newest building;, that same year the magazine won the National Magazine Award for general excellence. Surely then—since we know the exact time and place of its birth—the astrology chart should describe its progress, impact and growth over the decades.

National Geographic's Capricorn Sun is descriptive of its conservative, Earth-conscious and timeless image. People of all ages, from 8 to 108, children, to the elderly to yuppies and hippies are drawn to it. The Sun and Mercury, which is also in Capricorn, are conjunct in the 5th

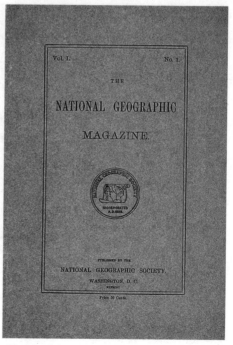

National Geographic Magazine first issue.

house. This shows a tie to leisure, learning and travel. In its own words *National Geographic* claims that it has transformed the rather dull subject of geography into a unique vision of the world, utilizing the talents of generations of men and women.

The tremendous wealth of the society (nearly all of it tax exempt) can be seen in the Capricorn placements in a trine aspect to the second house cusp (rules money) and to Neptune in Taurus at the midheaven. Including the Part of Fortune in Virgo, the chart shows a powerful and prosperous grand trine (wide orb) in the Earth signs (Taurus, Virgo and Capricorn). The Moon is in Aquarius, indicating an ideological and humanitarian connection to the public. Also this Moon sign describes the eccentric and adventurous lifestyles pursued

by those who work within the Society. Innovative and unpredictable as well as staunchly loyal, the staff of *National Geographic* is described by the Moon's 6th house position. *National Geographic* has provided information about the explorers of both the South and North Poles, the discovery and charting of the ancient city of Machu Picchu in Peru, inside visits to Castro's Cuba, Nazi Germany, as well as the 1969 Moon landing. It has retraced the routes of the early voyages of Christopher Columbus to the New World.

The Society's chart has Venus in Sagittarius and Jupiter in Scorpio, both in the fourth house. This hints at strong family ties. Since Gilbert Grosvenor became the first paid employee, reporting for work on April 1, 1899, the Grosvenor family has been linked

National Geographic editor, Gilbert H.Grosvenor at the headquarters in Washington, D.C.

The National Geographic Magazine 1905 logo.

to *National Geographic*. Control of its vast wealth and influence has been a family matter. Alexander Graham Bell, inventor of the telephone, was one of the original founders. With the marriage of Bell's daughter Elsie to Gilbert Grosvenor the Society assumed the mood of a dynasty. Its wealth and power remain in the hands of a close-knit group.

The strong tenth house in this chart is interesting. Pluto in early Gemini and Neptune at the very end of Taurus are there, in an out of sign conjunction. This combination of these two generational planets at the top of the horoscope describes global political and social power. *National Geographic* has always had close links to The White House. Its aims have frequently been sanctioned by United States Presidents. President Taft was a cousin of the Bell family, for example. Critics and conspiracy theory proponents claimed that Taft helped lend credibility to Robert E. Peary's claim to be the leader of the first expedition to reach the North Pole in 1909 when Dr. Frederick E. Cook claimed an earlier triumph. Controversies like this surround the Society, reflecting the explosive Pluto-Neptune influence in the sector of status and power.

The Mars-Uranus conjunction in Libra in the second house describes progressive technology. *National Geographic* pioneered the creative use of computers in producing documentaries, for example. This has always resulted in great financial gain.

Libra, being the sign of beauty combined with the pioneering spirit of Mars and Uranian originality is an eloquent astrological statement about the marvelous color photos which *National Geographic* is famous for. The Libra planets form a (wide orb) grand trine in air signs with the Moon in Aquarius and Pluto in Gemini. The double grand trines in both Earth and Air signs create a rare and beneficial Star of David aspect. Saturn, the ascendant and North Moon Node are all in Leo. A high quality of work, a flashy physical presence and leadership are shown here. The headquarters of the Society are richly decorated in Washington's most elegant district. One of the most significant points in this stunning chart is the mutual reception between the Sun in Capricorn and Saturn in Leo. The combination of influences there shouts enigmatic distinction combined with adventure and entertainment. A mutual reception (planets in each other's ruling signs) furnishes an almost magical ability to change places, to escape from whatever problems are gotten into. In the case of the Society, this certainly holds true. Close scrutiny of its history will bring scandals to light, yet the public image of *National Geographic* remains unscathed.

The twelfth house Saturn-Sun mutual reception describes the Society's focus on ecology and endangered species and an altruism toward third world cultures. The Society was formed on the day of a New Moon .In a horoscope which shows greatness, as this one does, a New Moon can indicate a universal symbolism. For example Queen Victoria, who was born on a New Moon, became the symbol for an entire age. *National Geographic* has this same kind of identity which makes further introduction unnecessary.

Perhaps it is enough just to say that there is only one *National Geographic*.

How to Interpret a Mundane Horoscope
When reading the horoscope of a city, nation, state, corporation, business, etc. the meanings of the houses and planets must be adjusted to expand beyond the familiar natal interpretations. Here is a guide to help you in working with this type of astrology:

The Sun: leadership, those persons in power, worldwide impact

The Moon: general public, changes, subordinates, history

Mercury: advertising, publications, educational value

Venus: profits, art, social functions

Mars: machinery, competition, adventure, turmoil, confrontations, danger

Jupiter: wealth, expansion, growth, success, philosophical values

Saturn: limitations, elderly people, archives, conservative values

Uranus: new technology, innovations, accidents

Neptune: inspiration, mystery, hidden factors, ghosts, paranormal activity

Pluto: power struggles, the masses, confidential information

Part of Fortune: luck and preferment

Chiron: guidance, balance of liberal with conservative viewpoints

North Moon Node: positive direction of aims

1st House (Ascendant or Rising Sign): morale, image, reputation

2nd House: assets, earnings, disposition of property

3rd House: traffic, inter-office communications, mail, neighborhood

4th House: foundation, heritage, origins

5th House: recreational facilities, younger people, the privileged

6th House: staff, working conditions, daily duties

7th House: competition, lawsuits, loyalties

8th House: treasury, debts, passing of power and assets from generation to generation.

9th House: foreign affairs, higher education, religion, travelers

10th House: highest authority, the boss, fame and fortune

11th House: fraternal spirit, politics, humanitarian endeavors

12th House: secrets, sorrows, undoing, isolation, karma, distant future

—DIKKI-JO MULLEN

132

NATIONAL GEOGRAPHIC

January 13, 1888, 8:00 PM in Washington, D.C.
(This "birth data" was obtained from The National Geographic Society,
100 years of Adventure and Discovery by C.D.P. Bryan.)

Data Table
Tropical Placidus Houses

Sun 23 Capricorn 21—5th House

Moon 1 Aquarius 50—6th House

Mercury 20 Capricorn 18—5th House

Venus 10 Sagittarius 42—4th House

Mars 18 Libra 18—2nd House

Jupiter 29 Scorpio 52—4th House

Saturn 3 Leo 51—12th House (retrograde)

Uranus 17 Libra 13—2nd House

Neptune 27 Taurus 25—10th House (retrograde)

Pluto 3 Gemini 14—10th House (retrograde)

North Moon Node 9 Leo 39—12th House

Part of Fortune 7 Virgo—1st House

Chiron 27 Gemini 49—10th House (retrograde)

Ascendant (rising sign) 28 Leo 36

Midheaven 23 Taurus 18

CAD GODDEU

The Battle of the Trees

MEDIEVAL historians concerned themselves with three great matters, these being the matters "of France, and of Britain, and of Rome the grand." The Matter of Britain is the body of literature, poetry, myth and legend that illuminates the life of old Gods, heroes and kings of Great Britain and Brittany. Much of the constituent histories, myths and poetry of the corpus survived in the ancient manuscripts—*The Black Book of Carmarthen, The Book of Taliesin, The Book of Aneirin* and *The Red Book of Hergest*—that William Forbes Skeen collected into a single manuscript called *The Four Ancient Books of Wales*. The individual manuscripts contained materials dating from as far back as the sixth century.

All the principals of *The Four Ancient Books of Wales* are important for their content, providing hints into the nature of a rich spoken body of literature. In the *The Book of Taliesin* is the enigmatic poem Cad Goddeu (The Battle of the Trees,) authored by Taliesin, the bard who according to legend was born of the enchantress Cerridwen.

Because of the poetic suggestive allusions and grammatically ambiguous style, translations varied widely. In 1858 David William Nash provided yet another translation. He believed that the poem was a single part of a larger Arthurian poetic track. He also believed that there was hidden lore to be gleaned from the poem, a theory he would abandon in due time. It was the Nash translation that

would eventually be accepted by many as the most accurate.

In the mid-1900s, Robert Graves, using the Nash tanslation, endeavored to interpret Cad Goddeu through a process of "correction," believing as Nash had that the poem contained hidden lore. He postulated that the poem's obtuse nature was a blind and that by reording the stanzas the true nature of the poem could be unlocked. Many modern Pagans became aquainted with the Graves translation by way of his book *The White Goddess*.

In short, the poem tellls of the battle between Gwydion and Arawn the lord of Annwn (the Otherworld.) The battle was instigated when the divine plowman Amaethon stole a dog, a lapwing and a roebuck from Arawn. While on first glance it seems as if the trees are sent into battle, it becomes evident at last that this is a battle of wits and that by guessing the name of Arawn's man Bran by the alder branches that he carried, the battle was won by Gwydion.

While the Graves' reimagining of The Battle of the Trees is considered by most scholars to be wishful insertion rather than accurate translation, there is certainly something to be gained from examining his text. He invigorated the poem through the insertion of some evocative ideas and also introduced meter in its English presentation. Certainly worthy of consideration by Pagans.

DEVON STRONG

134

The Battle of the Trees

Robert Graves after Taliesin

The tops of the beech tree
Have sprouted of late,
Are changed and renewed
From their withered state.

When the beech prospers,
Though spells and litanies
The oak tops entangle,
There is hope for the trees.

I have plundered the fern,
Through all secrets I spy,
Old Map ap Mathonwy
Knew no more than I.

For with nine sorts of faculty
God has gifted me:
I am fruit of fruits gathered
From nine sorts of tree -

Plum, quince, whortle, mulberry
Raspberry, pear,
Black cherry and white
With the sorb in me share.

From my seat at Fefynedd,
A city that is strong,
I watched the trees and green things
Hastening along.

Retreating fron happiness
They would fain be set
In forms of the chief letters
Of the alphabet.

Wayfarers wondered,
Warriors were dismayed
At renewal of conflicts
Such as Gwydion made:

135

Under the tongue root
A fight most dread,
And another raging
Behind, in the head.

The alders in the front line
Began the affray.
Willow and rowan-tree
Were tardy in array.

The holly, dark green,
Made a resolute stand;
He is armed with many spear points
Wounding the hand.

With foot-beat of the swift oak
Heaven and earth rung;
'Stout Guardian of the Door',
His name in every tongue.

Great was the gorse in battle,
And the ivy at his prime;
The hazel was arbiter
At this charmed time.

Uncouth and savage was the fir,
Cruel the ash tree -
Turns not aside a foot-breadth,
Staright at the heart runs he.

The birch. though very noble,
Armed himself but late:
A sign not of cowardice
But of high estate.

The heath gave consolation
To the toil-spent folk,
The long enduring poplars
In battle much broke.

Some of them were cast away
On the field of fight
Because of holes torn in them
By the enemy's might.

Very wrathful was the vine
Whose henchmen are the elms;
I exalt him mightily
To rulers of realms.

Strong chieftains were the blackthorn
With his ill fruit,
The unbeloved whitethorn (hawthorn)
Who wears the same suit.

The swift-pursuing reed,
The broom with his brood,
And the furze but ill-behaved
Until he is subdued.

The dower-scattering yew
Stood glum at the fight's fringe,
With the elder slow to burn
Amid fires that singe.

And the blessed wild apple
Laughing in pride
From the Gorchan of Maeldrew,
By the rock side.

In shelter linger
Privet and woodbine,
Inexperienced in warfare,
And the courtly pine.

But I although slighted
Because I was not big,
Fought, trees in your array
On the field of Goddeau Brig.

137

POLARITY
It's Not What You Think

THERE'S AN ENERGY that is one of the primary forces powering the universe—and all you have to do to access this power is stand there.

This is polarity as it was taught to me decades ago. Now let's unpack that concept and figure out what it means. Can polarity be meaningful to diverse people in the 21st century? As a queer woman, it mattered to me to find out and I hoped the answer was yes.

At its core, polarity is the interplay of energies between two forces that attract or repel. The Greek philosopher Empedocles considered love and strife—attraction and repulsion—to be divine powers that create all change and harmony in the universe. The Elements are static, he thought, but love and strife force them together and apart and this is the pulse of life.

Protons attract electrons and power your batteries. Erotic attraction creates life. Often, people in the occult say "gender polarity" as if that's the only kind. While gender is often a convenient label for polarity, the map should not be mistaken for the territory.

Visualize a pole: there's something at each end. North/South, black/white, active/passive—energy is generated whenever something moves along that pole. Things can and do move along it naturally but magicians can also push them along. The very existence of poles requires the existence of the entire area between them. If there is a North Pole and a South Pole, then by definition there must be an Equator. Polarity doesn't mean that people or things *are* any given pole, just that they exist somewhere in relation to the pole being discussed.

In alchemy, we find the very first polarity magic. *Solve et coagula*: break apart and bring together. Alchemy takes something—a metal, a plant, a human soul—breaks it into its component parts, purifies each part and brings it all back together in a pure form. Thus the original lead—dross, unexamined and undifferentiated—can be purified into gold. This process leverages polarity because every metal, plant and component part is assigned a gender. Alchemy, however, doesn't care about gender at all but only about breaking apart and coming back together. The goal is to find an ultimate oneness.

Over a thousand years later, 13th century Kabbalists defined polarity as the original force of creation. It was also Kabbalah that first took gender seriously—as in, polarities are not just labeled "male" and "female," but

138

are embodied. Polarity and sex magic first meet in Kabbalah.

All of this can easily read as queer. Alchemy wants you to take apart your ideas of opposites and put them back together as a single thing. Kabbalah finds that everything is also its opposite: *Geburah* is incomplete without *Chesed* and neither is truly whole until coming together to form *Tiferet*.

Obviously I'm simplifying but nonetheless we can look at the history of the occult and find in polarity a philosophical and magical concept that is both very ancient and kind of queer. We can call opposing forces—whether sulfur and mercury in Alchemy or mercy and justice in Kabbalah—"male" and "female," but the gender isn't straightforward and the ultimate magic is seeing that they're not different at all. I have a Hebrew tattoo on my arm that says *shamor v'zachor* (keep and remember.) In a Kabbalistic song, we're told that *shamor v'zachor* are two, but they are really one because God is One.

In the occult revival of the early 20th century the Golden Dawn and related groups stripped a lot of the queerness out of polarity and made the gender part both physical and essential. In a short time, this powerful universal magic came to be considered the product only of gendered bodies. Indeed, the force of polarity in this iteration exists merely by male and female practitioners working magic together. They don't even have to touch! This polarity, like I said, means just stand there.

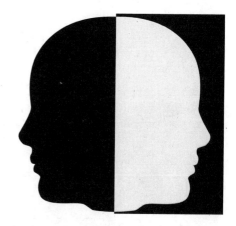

In the occult today, then, we have this idea that polarity is two people, one of whom is male and one female, working in an often ill-defined partnership in order to generate power, but that isn't necessarily the case.

I loved the process of uncovering the history of polarity, but academic study has its limits. I wanted to bring this knowledge back to my magical practice. As the queer high priestess of a majority-queer coven, I wanted to understand how polarity could be worked in the 21st century. It turns out to be fairly easy.

Polarity can be heterosexual, it can be gendered but queer and it can also be as non-gendered as sulfur and mercury. For example, a ritual of passive/active polarity has one partner hold each pole, forcing the passive partner to wait for the active partner in each ritual action.

Explorations like these can open our eyes to the power and complexity of polarity. Indeed, even if you're working a 100% heteronormative polarity, such experimentation can bring a power beyond "just stand there" to your magic.

—DEBORAH LIPP

EXPANDING CONSCIOUSNESS THROUGH VOCAL TONING

VOCAL TONING is the art of channeling energy through vocalization, a form of singing that focuses more on the energy created then the words or sounds being sung. The sound is long and drawn out in a similar fashion to singing opera or chanting *ohm*. The real key, however, lies in the Witch's ability to be open to the energy of the moment! When used as a tool for activating personal power and expanding consciousness, practitioners are able to connect through sound to the person, place or situation they are working on. Patience is recommended as—like most things—it requires practice. That being said, the experience of softening and reducing stress is often noticed the first time it is attempted, as the deep breathing and vibration of sound create a sense of calm similar to other meditative practices.

Magical working through vocalization is not a new practice. It has been used to communicate, enchant, soothe and command throughout time. Vocal toning with its hypnotic elongated vowel sounds draws you into a light to medium trance state. In this state of consciousness the Witch becomes the seeker, utilizing journey work, divination and healing for personal growth and understanding. While the journey often starts with the exploration of self, it often creates windows into the otherworld of spirit, as magic is not a linear study but instead a web of exploration!

When practicing vocal toning there are multiple ways to proceed. One of the simplest is to choose two or three simple sounds such as *hay-ho* or *ee-ah-oh*. Each syllable is drawn out (eeeeeeeee/ahhhhhhh/ohhhhh) over and over again in whatever pitch, tone or distortion comes through. This becomes a wordless song of sorts that will sound and feel different in different situations. Over time you will become sensitive to the differences in the sounds created and the information received in each experience. This free-form singing is often referred to as sacred singing because the experience is accompanied by a feeling of closeness and understanding. Every sacred song is different—there is no right way or wrong way to do sacred singing and in most instances the song ends naturally. However, if you are new to sacred singing and vocal toning, start with three to five minutes. When the you are ready to deepen your understanding of consciousness, it is helpful to stack the deck by incorporating techniques that enhance the experience such as consciously connecting with breath and toning power words and the names of sacred symbols.

Witches have long known the power of working with the Elements and vocal toning is no exception. Recognizing that the air entering your body is an elemental force is a powerful form of conscious breathing. The Element Air is connected to communication, inspiration, dreams and breath! When you recognize your work as a collaboration with the Spirit of Air, every inhalation is an invitation to the spirit to share itself and every exhalation an offering. You can incorporate this by simply taking a few moments to focus on breathing before starting a session or through a more elaborate technique in which you take a few moments to suck air through pursed lips, inhaling and exhaling consciously for a few breaths before starting.

After connecting with the Element Air and asking it to join the working, it is time to intone the names of magical symbols such as runes, reiki symbols and personal words of power. Activation through toning connects you to the energetic vibration of

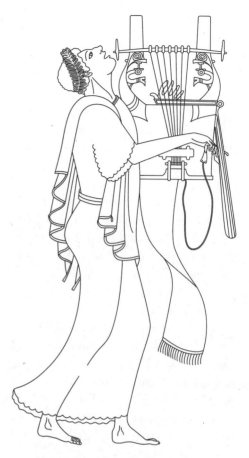

the word or symbol used. In this manner ordinary words from everyday vocabulary become powerful when intoned in spell work. Words such as "open," "love," "heal" and "grow" are powerful examples to explore. Like sacred singing, intoning symbols and words of power can be woven into a song—utilizing one or many—that will come to a natural end.

Over time, working with vocal toning provides the Witch with a quick method for expanding psychic sensitivity and altering consciousness as the mind becomes trained to enter a trance state through following the voice, making it a strong addition to any Witch's toolbox!

—SALI CROW

141

As Curandeiras da Ilha do Sol

The Healers from the Island of the Sun

The feeling of the smooth black basalt stones of the old 17th century cobbled streets underfoot is a poignant memory from childhood. These cobbles paved the road in the local village in Santa Maria, Azores. Known as the Island of the Sun because the rays of its first morning light touch her shores before any other island, the natural volcanic coastline and aquamarine gleaming waters evoke mystery. Azores is an archipelago located in the Macaronesia region of the North Atlantic and is an arrangement of nine islands in total. They belong to Portugal and were settled in the 17th century. A history of pirates, castles built of lava stone, tales of roaming spirits of seafarers and even sightings of mermaids enrich the local lore. Interestingly, legends have linked the Azores to the lost city of Atlantis. Perhaps the islands were once this lost civilization—magic certainly permeates through the land and its people.

Though Portugal is a Catholic country, its Pagan roots and traditions were—and still are—intertwined with the folk culture of the people. Since the 17th century, Azoreans (women primarily) have had strong ties with nature due to their socially expected domestic duties. Mothers teach daughters gardening, cooking, healing the sick and household chores. Men are taught husbandry and care for animals and the farms. Their traditional duties were outside the household but still tethered to the land. Many stories are passed down in families

142

by the women who experienced a rural, untouched Azores, about the recent time when they inhabited a world away from technology and modernity in a predominantly agricultural society in Santa Maria between the years 1957 and 1960.

Types of healers

Women at family gatherings often speak about the stories of the folk-healers or *curandeiras* (women-healers) or *curandeiros* (men-healers) who provided spiritual and medical aid to the islanders. Largely women-healers or curandeiras healed the ill, told fortunes, reversed bewitchment and removed curses. They were their own social group, seen by the majority as healers distinctly separate from midwives who would deliver children. Curandeiros, on the other hand, were spiritual leaders in the village when priests from other institutions like the Church could not provide spiritual guidance for unexplained events. They were well respected in the community and known for their efforts to care for villagers.

The majority of the healers were illiterate. Therefore, their practices were passed down generationally through family lines by an oral-based tradition. They were extremely sensitive to the spirit world and were able to drive out bewitchment from evil practitioners or *feiticeira*. It was common in this era in the region of the Santa Maria, Azores that the word "Witch" was not typically used. Rather, people used the vernacular Portuguese to describe Witchcraft or types of magic. For instance, "curandeiras" has in its prefix "*curar*," which means to heal. Therefore, "feiticeira" would be the opposition of curar through the use of maleficent forces since the prefix "*feit*" means to have done or to be fated. This implies a doomed or ill-fated situation, so if one became involved with a feiticeira they would do so at their own risk for doing so would often mean dealing with evil magic.

Perhaps both types of magic workers could be viewed as Witches or *buxas* as a matter of perspective as both beneficent and maleficent practices appear in folk beliefs. Villagers often thought when animals fell ill or when common cures had no effect that bewitchment had occurred, usually enacted by a feiticeira. Another possibility was the *cobranto*, which loosely translates to "the evil eye". This was seen as a type of curse due to the envy brought upon by a neighbor. In a village society, the more you climb the social ladder, the more conversation is stirred up among villagers regarding how families gain wealth, land and property. The more wealth you acquire, the more envy is brought upon you for your great fortune. In these situations, curandeiras might remove the envious curse with charms and fumigations.

Methods of healing and protection

Healing was usually a longer process. First, fortune telling would inform the client what exactly was ailing them spiritually. Unlike tarot or oracular-based divination techniques, a type of mediumship was used to sense bad-spirits, curses or the cobranto. It was then advisable to cleanse the person and household of entities or energy using a special kind of fumigation in a ceramic bowl or other vessel of herbs. Common herbs used for cleansing were *eucalipto* or eucalyptus for the lungs. *Alegrim* or rosemary was burned for general purification purposes as was *erva salvia* or sage. *Arrude* or rue was always tied to women's mysteries for it cured menstrual conditions. It was common for all families to have this

herb and it was also used to clear away the evil eye—the cobranto. In addition to these sacred plants, thyme was used for the lungs, cinnamon for diabetes, lemon balm for stomachache and nervousness and oregano for the lungs as well as small internal infections like colds. Teas were brewed for specific ailments since pharmaceuticals were not available in large quantities even as recently as the 50s and 60s. It would not be unlikely that a small cauldron would be used, since most homes in Santa Maria still had open hearths even into the twenty-first century!

Healers would use their own power—*força* or *poder*—to cleanse the energies of the house or the human body. Often older people speak of força or poder in reference to the workings of the curandeiras. This is a reference to the magical force or current that a magical worker holds within themselves. For the word "força" means "force," as in the force radiating from the practitioner to

144

expel negative energies. "Poder" literally means "to have" but more particularly in this context it means to have strong convictions in one's belief. Perhaps in the case of cleansing the healers use the power of will to make a change in their clients' spiritual environments.

At the time of birth, every child would be given a blessed amulet containing four sacred charms. Generally called *o signo* (charm,) the charm included the horn to give fertility and strength in life, a *figa*—symbol of a thumb folded between index and middle finder as a hand charm to ward off the evil eye, the pentacle for protection and in reference to the divine principle of man (macrocosm vs. microcosm) and, lastly, the Moon to ward off lunacy. The concept of the Moon is the most interesting since its purpose was to keep psychological health intact for the child, according to the belief that the Moon has great occult effect on the conditions of the mind.

Folk beliefs, death, saints and holy days
Festivals were often associated with the Catholic days, especially with saints' holy days. Close evaluation of these festivals suggests a link to older Pagan traditions in continental Europe. For instance, the celebration of Santa Amaro which took place on January 15th was particularly occult. If you broke an arm or leg within the year you would pray to St. Amaro for the limb to heal. You made a bargain with the saint, for if the limb healed fully on that saint's holy day you would bake bread in the shape of arms

and legs to sell out of your household to villagers. The money thus raised would go to the local church. In the classical era, gifts and sacrifices were offered to ancient Greek and Roman deities in a similar manner. The sacrifice is the creation of limb-shaped breads to pay homage to that saint for completing that magical task.

On November 1st, which was known as All Saints Day but called *Dia Dos Murtos* (Day of the Dead) in Santa Maria, church bells would ring in the evening, cleansing the gravesites and calling the villagers to pray for the dead. Death is inevitable and human mortality is constantly being interpreted through a variety of cultural traditions and beliefs. In Azorean village culture, if you died before your time or in a tragic accident it was believed that your spirit roamed. It was also believed that those spirits would likely have adverse effects on your family and their dwellings—therefore, the healer would be consulted for appropriate cleansings and prayers. Paying homage to the dead was also important to villagers, but it only occurred once a year. Only on the night of November 1st would people pray to their loved ones who had passed.

Saints were also highly regarded and petitioned for aid in everyday life. For instance, Santa Barbera was called upon against lightning or bad weather. Her festival was on December 4th but she was often prayed to like a deity to keep one's house and hearth protected when the rains and winds stirred.

The celebratory festival of *Senhora das Candeias*—which loosely translates to "the festival of the Lady of Light"—is known as Candlemas. Villagers would honor an enigmatic being of light—a symbol of the Virgin—and shape candles out of beeswax. They lit the candles and paraded around the village and into the church in the evening. This event marked the celebration of light and good fortune into the New Year. Interestingly, all villagers would participate, including the healers, for these practices were woven into their belief system.

Folk beliefs were common among all villagers in the community. Everyone was connected to old agricultural beliefs just as the healers or curandeiras were—the Earth provided all your resources and it was your main source of life. Even in the modern era, most houses had stone or compact dirt flooring. Very few people had the resources necessary to install indoor plumbing. Since homes did not have clocks, holes were placed strategically in between the mortar and brick—as the sun rose and set the holes would infer the time of the day as light shone through them in the wall.

Some of the lore passed down within families included agricultural folkways. For instance, all harvesting and planting occurs within the cycles of the Moon—you should always plant and prune before the Full Moon. There are special solar harvest and planting times for crops as well. For instance, corn is planted in January. If you see *raspa*—a painterly stroke of wisps in the clouds— prepare for strong gales the next day. Direct your attention to the stars, Moon and Sun for they are the clocks of the universe. Be careful with broken mirrors because they may provide you with years of bad luck. Never walk under a ladder for bad luck will follow. Always plant your sacred herbs in your garden and have rue bundled and dried in the household to avert the evil eye. Most of all, listen to your intuition for it never leads you astray.

—LUCIUS

146

Guru Rinpoche (Padmasambhava)

Hemis monastery in Leh, Ladakh,
Indian Controlled Jammu and Kashmir

Thumbs and Fingers of Green and Gold

THE THRILL of watching as a wrinkled seed turns into a colorful flower or as a scrawny seedling grows to produce luscious fruits and vegetables is an especially appealing and enduring kind of Witchery. Care, patience and selecting favorable planting dates combined with luck and just the right weather conditions will usually bring a degree of success in getting a garden to grow. Container gardens of herbs on balconies and backyard vegetable patches in housing developments are becoming an increasingly popular project for many who long for a connection with the land. There is an indescribable thrill in tasting a radish dug in one's own garden or in making a batch of apple butter from apples fresh from the tree in the corner of the backyard. Yet not all would-be growers have the same degree of success with their harvests. Even in times past some farmers would work hard only to fail miserably or enjoy only mediocre success while others would be the envy of neighbors and friends as their labors would produce amazing results, sometimes seeming almost effortless.

Over time this ability to charm plants has come to be described as "having a green thumb" in the United States. In Europe the gift is more often called "having green fingers." In the fairy tale "Jack and the Bean Stalk" of 1807, Jack seems to have a green thumb. This story alludes to the mystique of how a supernatural way with plants interfaces with the practice of magic and opens a whole new world. The name Jack hints at Jack in the Green or the Green Man, earlier beings who aligned with the Witchery of prolific greenery.

Recognition of the gift of a green thumb seems to date back at least to the year 1386 with the publication of the General Prologue to *The Canterbury Tales* by Geoffrey Chaucer. It might have originally been a gold thumb. Chaucer describes the Miller who "hadde a thombe of gold." Some linguists have interpreted this as the Miller's ability to select the finest golden wheat while others felt it indicated that the Miller was guilty of a greedy Midas-like approach in his business dealings. Another reference comes from the 1961 *Dictionary of Slang* by Eric Partridge. Partridge describes the slang as meaning that their gardening success comes from their personal affinity with plants.

The July 9, 1937 edition of *The Ironwood (Michigan) Daily Globe* cites "green thumb" in print, writing: "Besides being green eyed, Miss Dvorak has what is known as a 'green thumb.' That is horticultural slang for being a successful gardener with instinctive understanding of growing things."

That same summer *The Washington Post*, on June 6, 1937, also referenced the gift of being green thumbed: "He is, I think, the green thumbed type of gardener, who has lived and loved his flowers and has learned from them and from the soil. We've seen many theories for why the adjective green is used with both green thumbs and green fingers. The most common are that one's thumbs or other fingers are stained by handling mossy flowerpots or by pinching old blooms while deadheading."

An earlier reference to this gift comes from *Colour My Garden* by gardening writer Louise Beebe Wilder, which was published in 1918. Wilder wrote, "under the care of our green fingered grandmothers gardens throve and were full of hearty, wholesome colour."

In the eco-conscious world of the twenty-first century the word "green" expands to embrace an environmental application in showing love for plants with reverence, treasuring the precious gift of life itself. Think of green energy, a green economy, green space, etc.

—MARINA BRYONY

The Witchery of Lozen, A Medicine Woman

The Apache Joan of Arc

LOZEN was born about 1840 in an area in Taos County, New Mexico called Ojo Caliente, a place famous for its warm, healing mineral springs. She was and continues to be an exceptional personification of Goddess magic and warrioress shamanic power. The Apache band into which she was born, the Eastern Chiricahua, was matriarchal. The tribe's creation story honors a deity known as White Painted Woman. The role of medicine women is especially exalted in their culture. The Chiricahua (also called the Chihenne) Apache were formerly nomads. Their spiritual practices include painting their faces with ceremonial clay designs to bestow supernatural abilities. They called upon these forces historically for assistance in conducting raids and overcoming enemies.

From her childhood on Lozen—whose name means "dexterous horse thief"—showed astounding psychic talent. She battled to rid her homeland of invaders from Mexico as well as the United States and Europe. Lozen's life was completely dedicated to performing humanitarian acts of bravery to protect her people. Her military prowess was enhanced by her remarkable horsemanship and ability to shoot. Her brother was the famous

Apache Chief Victorio who was a trusted ally to and sometimes called the right hand man of the legendary Geronimo. After Victorio was killed, Lozen rode in battle with Geronimo. Historically Geronimo and Victorio are more well known but Lozen's story survives also. Victorio praised his sister, saying that Lozen was, "a shield to her people, strong as a man, braver than most and cunning in strategy." Her tireless dedication to others for more than thirty years coined her nickname, "the Apache Joan of Arc." Accounts describe Lozen as beautiful, a magnificent woman on horseback. Women often rode alongside the male warriors in her day, holding a knife or gun to assist. The Apache culture at that time did not believe in ownership, so stealing wasn't considered a crime. Stories are repeated today describing Lozen as a kind of Robin Hood figure. One involves her stealing a horse to help a new mother and her baby escape danger. Lozen is credited with often hiding children and elderly people in order to save their lives.

When locating an enemy, Lozen called upon magical and supernatural sources. Her gifts became active after she performed coming of age rites when

she went alone into the wilderness as an adolescent of about age 12. Reports document her talent for moving about unseen and disappearing into her surroundings. She was a prophetess who could find the direction of a potential enemy presence through her connection with a supreme Apache deity called Ussen. Tradition states that Ussen already existed at the dawn of time. He had no parents but sang four times—four is a sacred number among the Apache—to create life. He made both the first human being and a Sun God.

These two divine creations shook hands and the Earth appeared. It was too small at first so the pair kicked it around to gather more mass. As Earth grew larger Ussen created Tarantula to help. Tarantula did this by spinning a web with four cords which were then pulled to make the planet the right size. Afterwards, Ussen created the first tribes out of a sacred fire. He then left, but he still watches over humanity from the distant cosmos. Ussen might intercede to help from time to time, especially if called upon.

To gain his aid, Lozen would stand with her hands outstretched chanting an invocation to Ussen while slowly turning around in a circle. Then either her veins would turn dark blue or her palms would begin to tingle. Either reaction would reveal the significant direction as Ussen's answer. In her chant, Lozen named Ussen's power over the Earth, and then claimed that power for herself for her specific purposes.

Lozen never had a commitment ceremony like a marriage to a man recorded. She did have a longtime female companion and there is some speculation

Prisoner of war photo of Lozen

about the nature of this relationship. The Apache recognized several, maybe as many as seven, different gender identifications. After years of warfare and the death of Victorio, Lozen assisted other Native Americans in the brokering of a peace treaty to free about 600 Native Americans who were being held prisoner. It was an agreement of surrender and the laying down of arms. As is true of every other treaty, the government would break the agreement with the Native Americans. Five days later Lozen was among a group, including Geronimo, who were transported by train to Florida and then to the Mount Vernon Barracks in Alabama. She died there—probably of dysentery or tuberculosis—on June 17, 1889 at about age fifty. Some members of her tribe eventually managed to return West to their ancestral lands in New Mexico, where Lozen is still honored. Storytellers maintain an oral tradition remembering her exploits to this day.

—GRANIA LING

151

Moon Cycles

A New Moon rises with the Sun,
Her waxing half at midday shows,
The Full Moon climbs at sunset hour,
And waning half the midnight knows.

NEW	2025	FULL	NEW	2026	FULL
		Jan 13			Jan 3
Jan 29		Feb 12	Jan 18		Feb 1
Feb 27		Mar 14	Feb 17		Mar 3
Mar 29		Apr 12	Mar 18		Apr 1
Apr 27		May 12	Apr 17		May 1
May 26		June 11	May 16		May 31**
June 25		July 10	June 14		June 29
July 24		Aug 9	July 14		July 29
Aug 23		Sept 7	Aug 12		Aug 28
Sept 21		Oct 6	Sept 10		Sept 26
Oct 21		Nov 5	Oct 10		Oct 26
Nov 20		Dec 4	Nov 9		Nov 24
Dec 19			Dec 8		Dec 23

*A rare second New Moon in a single month is called a "Black Moon."
**A rare second Full Moon in a single month is called a "Blue Moon."

Life takes on added dimension when you match your activities to the waxing and waning of the Moon. Observe the sequence of her phases to learn the wisdom of constant change within complete certainty.

Dates are for Eastern Standard and Daylight Time.

152

presage

by Dikki-Jo Mullen

ARIES, 2024–PISCES, 2025

THE CELESTIAL picture for the coming year promises incredible and unprecedented changes. Coping with it all while nurturing enthusiasm, the precious urge to forge a personal world of freedom and empowerment, is the goal of this year's Witches' Almanac. In Presage can be found an astrological guide to finding the path through self care. The goal is to encourage readers to aspire to loftier heights. Spiritual studies can help to bring this about. Each person dwells in a self-created universe. What is willed and focused upon is what manifests. This year's Presage accents living/dying, healing, growth, overcoming obstacles, and more.

Pluto, the celestial transformer, transits Aquarius. Uranus, the indicator of progress and surprises, is joined by expansive and benevolent Jupiter in Taurus. Serious Saturn, the planet of parameters and karma, moves with dreamy and otherworldly Neptune in Pisces. Five eclipses

punctuate this year's important cosmic message. The rare total solar eclipse on April 8, 2024 will be especially significant. Called "The Ring of Fire", this much anticipated eclipse will darken the sky, blocking the Sun all across North America beginning in Mexico, with its shadow continuing over the United States to finally exit over Newfoundland and Prince Edward Island, Canada. (This is being called the most significant cosmic event since "The Great American Eclipse" of August 21, 2017, which spanned the contiguous USA from coast to coast.)

To understand what this means to you first consult the forecast for your Sun sign, the familiar birth sign and the most significant single factor in the birth chart. Next consult the forecasts for your Moon sign and ascendant (rising sign). The Moon sign forecast explores memories and emotions. The ascendant describes personal appearance, how others see you. Here begins Presage.

ASTROLOGICAL KEYS

Signs of the Zodiac
Channels of Expression

ARIES: fiery, pioneering, competitive
TAURUS: earthy, stable, practical
GEMINI: dual, lively, versatile
CANCER: protective, traditional
LEO: dramatic, flamboyant, warm
VIRGO: conscientious, analytical
LIBRA: refined, fair, sociable
SCORPIO: intense, secretive, ambitious
SAGITTARIUS: friendly, expansive
CAPRICORN: cautious, materialistic
AQUARIUS: inquisitive, unpredictable
PISCES: responsive, dependent, fanciful

Elements

FIRE: Aries, Leo, Sagittarius
EARTH: Taurus, Virgo, Capricorn
AIR: Gemini, Libra, Aquarius
WATER: Cancer, Scorpio, Pisces

Qualities

CARDINAL	FIXED	MUTABLE
Aries	Taurus	Gemini
Cancer	Leo	Virgo
Libra	Scorpio	Sagittarius
Capricorn	Aquarius	Pisces

CARDINAL signs mark the beginning of each new season — active.
FIXED signs represent the season at its height — steadfast.
MUTABLE signs herald a change of season — variable.

Celestial Bodies
Generating Energy of the Cosmos

Sun: birth sign, ego, identity
Moon: emotions, memories, personality
Mercury: communication, intellect, skills
Venus: love, pleasures, the fine arts
Mars: energy, challenges, sports
Jupiter: expansion, religion, happiness
Saturn: responsibility, maturity, realities
Uranus: originality, science, progress
Neptune: dreams, illusions, inspiration
Pluto: rebirth, renewal, resources

Glossary of Aspects

Conjunction: two planets within the same sign or less than 10 degrees apart, favorable or unfavorable according to the nature of the planets.

Sextile: a pleasant, harmonious aspect occurring when two planets are two signs or 60 degrees apart.

Square: a major negative effect resulting when planets are three signs from one another or 90 degrees apart.

Trine: planets four signs or 120 degrees apart, forming a positive and favorable influence.

Quincunx: planets are 150 degrees or about 5 signs apart. The hand of fate is at work and unique challenges can develop. Sometimes a karmic situation emerges.

Opposition: a six-sign or 180° separation of planets generating positive or negative forces depending on the planets involved.

The Houses — *Twelve Areas of Life*

1st house: appearance, image, identity
2nd house: money, possessions, tools
3rd house: communications, siblings
4th house: family, domesticity, security
5th house: romance, creativity, children
6th house: daily routine, service, health

7th house: marriage, partnerships, union
8th house: passion, death, rebirth, soul
9th house: travel, philosophy, education
10th house: fame, achievement, mastery
11th house: goals, friends, high hopes
12th house: sacrifice, solitude, privacy

Eclipses

Elements of surprise, odd weather patterns, change and growth are linked to eclipses. Those with a birthday within three days of an eclipse can expect some shifts in the status quo. There will be five eclipses this year, two are total and three are partial.

March 25, 2024—Full Moon—partial lunar eclipse in Libra, South Node

April 8, 2024—New Moon—total solar eclipse in Aries, North Node

September 17, 2024—Full Moon—partial lunar eclipse in Pisces, North Node

October 2, 2024—New Moon—partial solar eclipse in Libra, South Node

March 14, 2025—Full Moon—total lunar eclipse in Virgo, South Node

A total eclipse is more influential than a partial. The eclipses conjunct the Moon's North Node are thought to be more favorable than those conjunct the South Node.

Retrograde Planetary Motion

Retrogrades promise a change of pace, different paths and perspectives.

Mercury Retrograde

Impacts technology, travel and communication. Those who have been out of touch return. Revise, review and tread familiar paths. Affected: Gemini and Virgo

April 1–25, 2024
in Aries

August 4–28, 2024
in Virgo and Leo

November 25, 2024–December 15, 2024
in Sagittarius

March 15, 2025–April 7, 2025
in Pisces and Aries

Venus Retrograde

Venus retrograde influences art, finances, and love. Affected: Taurus and Libra

March 1, 2025–April 12, 2025
in Pisces and Aries

Mars Retrograde

The military, sports, and heavy industry are impacted. Affected: Aries and Scorpio.

December 6, 2024–February 23, 2025
in Cancer and Leo

Jupiter Retrograde

Large animals, speculation, education, and religion are impacted. Affected: Sagittarius and Pisces

October 9, 2024–February 4, 2025
in Gemini

Saturn Retrograde

Elderly people, the disadvantaged, employment and natural resources are linked to Saturn. Affected: Capricorn and Aquarius

June 29, 2024–November 15, 2024
in Pisces

Uranus Retrograde

Inventions, science, electronics, revolutionaries and extreme weather relate to Uranus retrograde. Affected: Aquarius

September 1, 2024–January 30, 2025
in Taurus

Neptune Retrograde

Water, aquatic creatures, chemicals, spiritual forces and psychic phenomena are impacted by this retrograde. Affected: Pisces

July 2, 2024–December 7, 2024
in Pisces

Pluto Retrograde

Ecology, espionage, birth and death rates, nuclear power and mysteries relate to Pluto retrograde. Affected: Scorpio

May 2, 2024–October 11, 2024
in Aquarius and Capricorn

ARIES
March 20–April 19
Spring 2024–Spring 2025 for those
born under the sign of the Ram

Enterprising, quite social and bold, this Mars ruled fire sign is all about firsts. Aries is first to make wants and needs known and first to explore new options. Aries moves onward and upward. There is often resistance, though, if a suggestion is presented too forcefully. You prefer to take the initiative and create something new rather than following standard procedure. Your focus is always on the future. Rehashing the past tends to bore you.

Mercury influences Aries from the Spring Equinox until May 15. This entire time favors study, travel and communication. During most of April Venus moves along with Mercury through your 1st house, stimulating creative expression, love and artistic appeal. By May Day your financial sector is affected by the Sun and Uranus. Explore how current trends might impact your income. Create an emergency fund to anticipate future financial needs. A vibrant Mars influence inspires a competitive spirit during May and early June. Your enthusiasm peaks near June 8.

Mid-June through July 10 Venus brightens your sector of home and family life. Redecorate, entertain at home and welcome guests near the Summer Solstice. The last three weeks of July accent transportation needs and keeping up with current events. Dedicate an altar and seasonal ritual at Lammas to wellness. Your health sector is active during the waning weeks of summer. This supports exploring new dietary and fitness modalities. August 30–September 20 a strong Venus aspect brings good fortune to a close partner. Revel in the success and recognition achieved by another. Celebrate the Autumn Equinox by sharing a feast of seasonal fruits and veggies. Visualize manifesting mutual dreams and goals. The Full Moon in Aries on October 17 moves relationships to a new level. Late October through All Hallows finds your attention turning toward research and problem solving. Enjoy reading a good mystery story during the cool evenings. Within the pages a favorite character inspires your Halloween costume.

Throughout November and early December several planetary patterns turn your attention toward faraway places and new horizons. This could indicate travel, a new spiritual direction or even an interest in trying a new job or hobby. The time span of November 25–December 5 reveals the specifics. Mars, your ruler, begins a retrograde cycle December 6. This hovers in the background of your life until late February. Repeating patterns bring recurring dejavu during this entire time. Loved ones, ancestry and enjoyable pastimes can intertwine with this. The New Moon on December 30 will offer clarity concerning this trend. At the Winter Solstice new goals emerge, perhaps encouraged by activities suggested by friends. Prepare a treasure map or vision board on the shortest of days to illustrate your preferred path for

156

the future. By January 3 Venus joins Saturn and Neptune in your 12th house. Charitable gestures bring solace throughout January. You would find satisfaction in assisting those less fortunate. This could include rescuing animals in need. The middle of January can be especially hectic. A strong mutable sign emphasis, especially involving Jupiter, promises a busy schedule then which demands multitasking. From January 21 through mid-February helpful people will be available to offer assistance. Don't try to do everything alone. On February 4 Venus enters Aries, where it will remain through the end of the winter. More appreciation and support will come your way. A cycle of improvement in relationships of all kinds commences, along with more promising financial situations. Mars completes its retrograde on February 23. Your motivation and energy level will improve dramatically. March finds you completing repairs and various home improvement projects. Real estate transactions can be successful during this time.

HEALTH

As a step in self care try a boxing workout. Boxing is wonderful for both physical fitness and emotional release of stress. Your strength and sense of power will move to a whole new level. Taking preventative health measures and maintaining wholesome habits is especially important this year. The eclipses in Aries on April 8, 2024 and March 14, 2025 will reveal how long-term health choices have affected your overall wellness.

LOVE

Surprising developments are likely to occur regarding a close relationship this year. There could be an ending or a new beginning impacting your journey toward true love. Venus transits your birth sign in the spring, starting on April 5, and again in late winter, starting on February 4, highlighting romantic bliss. Make a Valentine's Day date memorable and charm the one you would woo.

SPIRITUALITY

Saturn and Neptune in your 12th house indicate that solitary times of contemplative reflection can enhance spirituality this year. Out of the peace and quiet grows a deeper connection with the Lord and Lady. Volunteer work and charitable activities to benefit those less fortunate hold unique potential for spiritual growth this year. Spiritual awakening is especially likely near the lunar eclipse on September 17 or during at Candlemas on February 1–2. Light a purple candle to stimulate spiritual insights.

FINANCE

Uranus is in the midst of a long-term passage of many years in your 2nd house of money. Fluctuations in both cash flow and source of income have probably taken you on something of a financial roller coaster ride. Jupiter, often an indicator of luck and wealth, will join Uranus in your money sector from the Spring Equinox through May 25. Cultivate financial opportunities then. A stroke of luck can turn finances for the better, even bringing a windfall.

157

TAURUS
April 20–May 20
Spring 2024–Spring 2025 for those
born under the sign of the Bull

Genuine, practical and patient, this earth sign usually delights in connecting with nature. Taureans are often gifted gardeners. With stoic determination, a devoted and sometimes obstinate nature, you have a way of nearly always getting what you want. Ruled by Venus, you insist upon quality and will seek the finest things that life has to offer. This can include purchasing the best fashions, jewels, art and gourmet foods. Your love of beauty extends to include pleasant sounds and a dislike of noise pollution. Music, especially singing, can be important to you.

At the Spring Equinox Venus highlights your 11th house, promising harmonious interactions with friends. Accept invitations. You might become more active in a civic or social organization during April. On May Day Jupiter, Venus and the Sun are all in your birth sign. This is a bright, benevolent influence, relationships deepen. Fill May baskets with flowers and candy to surprise those you admire. A positive time of healing and growth continues through May 25. During the first half of June Mercury will transit your 2nd house of finances. A business trip can be lucrative near the New Moon on June 6. Thoughts and conversations will revolve around money matters. June brings an excellent time to study and gather information about finances. At the Summer Solstice the Sun, Mercury and Venus impact your 3rd house. Bless a citrine crystal or seashell as a talisman for travel. Your schedule will be punctuated by a number of errands and short journeys. A helpful neighbor initiates casual conversation and reaches out in friendship.

The first three weeks of July brings a strong Mars influence. Your energy level will be high. Motivation and a competitive attitude spur you forward. Avoid upsetting a sensitive person as the Full Moon on July 21 draws near. Control anger with a bit of humor and tolerance. Mercury trines your Sun July 27–August 14. Others share interesting perspectives and opinions near Lammastide. Visit a bookstore or historic site. A favorable Venus transit in mid to late August opens the door to enjoyable recreational activities. You are glad about a young person's growth and accomplishments. September 1–8 a tense Mercury influence brings several projects which require immediate attention. Pace yourself and prioritize. As the Autumn Equinox nears your health is the focus. Enjoy seasonal fruits and vegetables to feel lighter in body and spirit. From late September through October 17 Venus will oppose your Sun. The choices of another can be at odds with your preferences. Tolerance helps resolve a conflict. At All Hallows cover comfortable, casual clothing with a beautiful cape. Share favorite ghost stories discuss psychic experiences.

During November plans and suggestions offered by others set the pace.

Teamwork and partnerships mold the flow of events. The Full Moon on November 15 brings this trend to a peak and finds you feeling ready to be more assertive in making choices. Winter holiday plans are involved in this pattern. The retrograde Mercury cycle of November 25–December 15 affects your 8th house. Messages from the spirit realm and memories of times long past surface. Solving an old mystery is involved. At the Winter Solstice divine the truth with the Tarot or a pendulum. Late December through January 5th a Mars influence brings the need for adjustments regarding your family dynamics. A house blessing might help to balance any discordant energies. The 2nd and 3rd weeks of January bring a refreshing Mercury transit in your 9th house. Your thoughts take a philosophical turn. Try journaling as well as initiating discussions. A book club or writers' group could be worth attending. As February begins others will express security concerns. Help by being a caring listener. On Candlemas burn white candles to enhance faith.

Jupiter completes its retrograde on February 4 in your 2nd house of finances. An old obligation is resolved, enabling a financial goal to be within reach. During the last half of February a strong 11th house influence stimulates altruism. At the New Moon on February 27 make choices which can benefit the Earth as well as the quality of life for those less fortunate. On March 1 Venus turns retrograde in your 12th house. Past life memories can be understood and processed. You are freed of regrets and disappointments.

HEALTH
The eclipses on March 25 and October 2 indicate the need to be flexible regarding your wellness agenda. A health care professional offers valuable insights. Self care for you can be enhanced by connecting with nature. Relax near the water. Listen to waves hitting the shore, a stream rushing over rocks or birds singing. Enjoy the sensual feeling and fragrance of fallen leaves and grasses to feel less stressed. If going outside is impractical try listening to recordings of nature sounds.

LOVE
May and August bring favorable Venus influences, promising romantic interludes. You tend to cling to love interests. Sometimes it's important to recognize when it's time to move on. The eclipse on March 14, 2025 is a time to consider whether a romantic connection has run its course. A totally new love interest could replace the old at that time.

SPIRITUALITY
The Full Moon on June 21 brings spiritual awakening. Combine a drawing down ritual with observances for the solstice to experience meaningful insights. Release a toxic situation. And advance spiritually.

FINANCE
You can be so concerned about financial security that you forget to enjoy the blessings you have. Practice an attitude of gratitude. Jupiter transiting Taurus promises greater abundance in the springtime, near your birthday.

GEMINI
May 21–June 20
Spring 2024–Spring 2025 for those
born under the sign of the Twins

Versatile and multifaceted, Gemini has perfected the art of flexibility, adapting to the whim of the moment. Others might even say that you appear different, almost unrecognizable, at different times. This flair for shape-shifting extends beyond your appearance to include personality traits and behaviors. The mercurial Twins are charming and intriguing, yet can be puzzling and exasperating too. Ruled by Mercury, Gemini is usually gifted with exceptional communication skills.

The Spring Equinox finds Venus in your 10th house, setting the pace until April 4. Your creativity and social skills open the way for success. Mercury will be retrograde during most of April. Your preferences can waver regarding your goals and aspirations. Somehow you'll revisit the past. A reunion might be planned. May begins with a yearning for peace and privacy. Several placements emphasize your 12th house. Insights come following a dream or meditation on either May Day or near the New Moon on May 7. During mid-May a Saturn influence can make the daily grind, your workload, seem heavy. Patiently keep trying. Do what you can. Venus transits Gemini, bringing greater love and

appreciation your way May 24–mid-June. Shop for jewelry, fashions or home décor items near your birthday. By the Summer Solstice lucky Jupiter will conjoin your Sun. Pursue opportunities for growth. A wish is fulfilled. On the longest of days practice affirmations related to a cherished goal.

From the last week of June through July 20 your money sector is activated. Heed information which comes your way regarding finances. This is an optimum time to perfect salable job skills and update a resume. Mars enters your 1st house on July 21, a trend which lasts until September 4. During this entire time your motivation will be high and your elevated vitality and enthusiasm will be a catalyst for adventure. Dedicate a Lammas rite to the release of anger or stress and summer's waning days will be very memorable and exciting.

A Mercury aspect comes into play September 9–25 can make you a bit chatty and indiscreet. Think things through before making a hasty choice or voicing controversial opinions. At the Autumn Equinox meditate on options. A friend offers a new perspective on available choices. The eclipse on October 2 highlights your sector of leisure, romance and pleasure. A new hobby or love interest is likely to arise near Halloween. Consider a colorful costume, perhaps a gypsy look. Add beads, scarves and other decorative touches.

November begins with a Venus opposition. This trend remains until November 11. A companion might have different preferences and tastes. Compromise to maintain a happy

160

relationship. Keep a tolerant attitude regarding love. Allow someone close to you to be themselves. The New Moon on December 1 is in your 7th house of partnerships. A commitment enters a new phase, allowing you to adjust for the role another will or won't play in your life. The retrograde Mercury during the first half of December reveals patterns in relationships. The past holds valuable clues which can guide you in planning for the present and future.

The Full Moon on December 15 awakens the spirit of the winter holidays. Decorate and prepare for the solstice. On the longest of nights destiny speaks to you during a time of reverie or revelry. From late December through January 2 a philosophical mood prevails. Seasonal stories and legends have personal relevance. From mid-January until Candlemas Venus transits your midheaven. This is a time when expressing kindness and good manners enhances your reputation. Coworkers can be affected by the personal dramas in their lives. On February 2 light a yellow candle to Brigid for help in understanding a troubled individual. Mid-February finds Mercury creating a stir in your schedule. There might be many distractions and interruptions to cope with. How can you minimize this? On February 23 Mars changes direction in your financial sector. You will find a way to move past frustrations or blockages related to money matters as February ends. During March sentimental recollections are stimulated by retrograde Venus. Someone from the past reaches out.

HEALTH
From the end of May through the remainder of the entire year Jupiter will be in Gemini. This brings potential for real progress in overcoming ongoing health challenges. Yet, Jupiter's powerful influence can indicate extremes. Maintain a wholesome moderation regarding fitness programs and dietary choices. In approaching self care remember to laugh and lighten up. A sense of humor can be a real asset in maintaining wellness.

LOVE
The eclipses on March 25 and October 2 both affect your 5th house of love and romance. Love connections can begin, end or grow near those dates. Venus, the love goddess among the planets, smiles on you in June and September.

SPIRITUALITY
Travel to sacred sites expands your spiritual horizons. Visit places of spiritual or historic significance near the Full Moons on July 21 and August 19. You might follow multiple spiritual paths or change your spiritual path several times during your life. The study of comparative religions can enhance your spiritual awareness.

FINANCE
Mars transits your money sector September 5–November 3 and again from January 6 through the end of the winter. This brings a need to make extra effort in order to meet financial goals. Benevolent Jupiter's presence in Gemini for most of the year assures profits in the long run. Winter brings a satisfactory conclusion regarding finances.

161

CANCER

June 21–July 22

Spring 2024–Spring 2025 for those
born under the sign of the Crab

Fastidious and sentimental, the Crab conceals a vulnerable interior psyche beneath its tough outer shell. History, including memories related to family life and heritage, are cherished. You like keepsakes and might assemble impressive arrays of collectibles. Cancerians are diplomats with a unique ability to relate to those much younger or older. Considerate and hospitable, you like to make certain that others are comfortable and well fed.

At the Spring Equinox hints of changes in family dynamics develop near the eclipse on March 25. This eclipse activates your 4th house, the sector of heritage and home. A move could be considered. During April retrograde Mercury sets the pace. There can be some loose ends and old business to complete regarding a career situation. Verify appointments and instructions in order to keep things moving smoothly at work. Reflect on past patterns. It is worthwhile to draw upon experience during April for valuable insights. On May Day Venus, Jupiter and the Sun brighten your 11th house. This favors gathering with friends. Honor loved ones by letting them know that your thoughts are with them. News and invitations are shared throughout May. The New Moon on May 7 is a time to make plans, especially involving travel. From late May to mid-June a strong 12th house influence brings a yearning for peace and privacy. You will find solace in quietly doing good deeds for the benefit those in need. At the Full Moon on the Summer Solstice animal companions will be an especially important part of your life. Consider adopting a new cat, dog, bird or bunny then.

July 1–25 a Mercury transit in your 2nd house turns the focus toward finances as the primary topic of conversations. Sharpen salable job skills then and pursue new sources of income. Late July through August 3 you'll seek peace and simplicity. Plan a picnic to celebrate Lammas. Share a platter of seasonal fruits with a selection of cheeses. Near the New Moon on August 4 transportation needs are addressed. Throughout the remainder of August others look to you for advice and inspiration. September begins with a week-long shopping spree. A stimulating Sun aspect awakens an urge to replace worn out wardrobe items and replenish your pantry in preparation for the new season. Mars enters Cancer on September 5. This dynamic transit sets a busy and competitive pace until early November. By the Autumn Equinox, near September 23, you may find yourself in a position of leadership. Dedicate a seasonal fall ritual to unity and anger release.

The solar eclipse on October 2 emphasizes changing roles within the family. A loved one shares a secret. Venus moves through your 5th house September 23 through October 17. You are surrounded by love. There will be opportunities to

162

share leisure time activities as well as creative projects or a romantic interlude with a dear one. Halloween week brings a dynamic Mercury transit. An impromptu journey is rewarding. It's a good time to stop by a favorite bookstore or library. A literary character inspires your costume choice.

During November Mercury highlights your health sector. Prepare wholesome and delicious foods. Enjoy the fresh air and get some exercise to strengthen both the mind and body. Others offer worthwhile health-related thoughts. On December 1 the New Moon favors making changes in your daily schedule to facilitate comfort and well-being. Mars begins a retrograde cycle on December 6 which affects money matters throughout the winter holiday season. Compare prices and avoid impulse buying. At the Winter Solstice burn bayberry candles as a prosperity charm. Visit a resale or thrift store to find a bargain or treasure in early December. January brings a focus on both business and personal partnerships. The Full Moon on January 13 offers insights into how associates view you.

The last half of January brings a favorable Venus influence in your 9th house. The art, music and cuisine of other lands call to you now. At Candlemas include an unusual lantern or folk art accent to your altar. In February Jupiter turns direct in your 12th house. You can heal from and release nagging regrets or bad memories. The Full Moon on February 12 reinforces your sense of security. March brings favorable water sign influences. Interpret dreams and impressions received during meditation.

The information might be communication from angels and spirit guides.

HEALTH

A waterfront stroll or an afternoon of boating can often reinforce both your mental and physical wellness. Controlling stress and anger is essential from September until early November and again from January 26 through winter's end. Those are times when Mars will conjoin your Sun. For some quick self care bake a loaf of homemade bread. The wholesome aroma and time spent kneading and preparing the dough followed by having a fresh snack ready promises a nurturing experience.

LOVE

June 17–July 11 marks a Venus transit through Cancer. This supports love connections near your birthday. Wear or carry a moonstone during the Full Moons on April 23 and January 13 to facilitate romantic encounters.

SPIRITUALITY

Saturn and Neptune will remain in your 9th house all year. This pattern favors spiritual growth through regular meditation and ritual observances as well as through the study of spiritual literature. Journaling offers a wonderful tool in monitoring spiritual growth throughout the year.

FINANCE

Jupiter will sextile your Sun from the Spring Equinox through May 25. This fortunate aspect has the potential to generate worthwhile financial opportunities and business connections. Cultivating these should encourage monetary success.

LEO
July 23–August 22
Spring 2024–Spring 2025 for those
born under the sign of the Lion

Ruled by the Sun, the Lion shines. You have a debonair and regal presence. With natural warmth and self confidence and enthusiasm, you have a flair for combining business with pleasure. You are playful, generous and young at heart yet dignified. Always you appreciate quality.

The springtime begins with Mercury in your 9th house. Travel is appealing and you are in the mood for adventure and exploration. Expect a change of direction and new possibilities. Mid to late April finds Mars and Saturn affecting finances, especially investment strategies. Be patient and select low-risk options. On May Day a Venus transit in your 10th house begins. This brings social and friendship factors into your professional environment through May 23. Focus on making colleagues feel comfortable and the workplace more attractive. By June a Jupiter transit in your 11th house gains momentum. Your network of acquaintances is expanding. Promises made and shared dreams affect your role within an important organization. At the Summer Solstice involvement in group activities will be more than enough of a good thing. You will seek more independence. July 1–25 Mercury in Leo stimulates your mind. New publi-

cations, a class or educational travel can be appealing. Facilitate a roundtable discussion at Lammas. Exchange ideas with those who have different viewpoints. The New Moon in Leo on August 4 brings a fresh perspective concerning your priorities. The remainder of August finds you juggling finances. Solutions arise after Mercury retrograde is over on August 28.

September 1–22 brings a pleasant influence from Venus in your sector of communication. An encouraging conversation with a neighbor or sibling brightens summer's last days. This is a good time to catch up on correspondence or a writing project. At the Autumn Equinox spruce up your front door with decorative accents. How about assembling a wreath of autumn colored leaves, acorns and grasses? Or a terra-cotta planter of gold and red chrysanthemums? October 1–13 a series of short errands keeps you on the go. Address transportation needs. The last half of October through November 11 finds Venus brightening your 5th house of leisure activities and romance. You can enjoy attending sports events or trying a craft project. Host a Halloween gathering. Award prizes for the best costumes.

Mars enters Leo in early November. This trend continues until early January. Although it sparks motivation and enthusiasm, Mars also can generate conflict, anger and impatience. Direct efforts and energy in positive, constructive ways. The New Moon on November 1 is a good time to address housing needs and family dynamics. Mid-November–December 6 Venus transits your 6th house. Loving animal companions attract happiness and magic to everyday life. This is a good time to celebrate the seasonal holidays with coworkers. It's also favorable for reaching out to a special cousin, nephew or auntie. As the Winter Solstice approaches several influential retrograde planets, including Jupiter and Mars, suggest second chances. This might mean repairing a broken relationship or rekindling an abandoned dream. Nostalgia can be especially heavy near the Full Moon on December 15. Display vintage ornaments and old photos for reminiscing. While honoring the longest of nights include fragrance in a ritual. Pine or apple and cinnamon aromas would be good choices for attracting prosperity and congenial spirits.

January ushers in health considerations. Be aware of the need for adequate sleep. Limit contact with those who are unwell. You might be vulnerable to picking up a passing "bug," especially near the Full Moon on January 13. By Candlemas your vitality will improve. Celebrate the holiday by lighting three red candles. Near February 12, at the Full Moon in Leo, conversations and messages are pivotal. Heed what others are communicating. During late February Mars stations in your 12th house. You will savor solitude, freed from the drama and distractions others can generate. The wisdom of keeping silent is underscored. During March Sun, Saturn and Neptune transits in your 8th house can indicate contact with the afterlife including interaction with elementals, such as the elves and other fey ones. These spirit visitors are loving and caring. Interpret your dreams

during winter's final days, because an omen or message will be revealed.

HEALTH
This year Saturn and Neptune are quincunx your Sun. Fate and heredity will impact health. Explore the parameters of your own endurance levels. For self care draw upon the natural energies of the mineral kingdom. Carry a medicine bag of high vibration stones with you to assure high vibes always. Amber, peridot, leopard jasper and tiger's eye agate are all excellent choices.

LOVE
Two Full Moons will be significant regarding your love connections this year. The Full Moon on May 23 affects your sector of romance. The Full Moon on August 19 highlights a serious commitment to a soulmate. Venus will transit Leo July 11–August 4. That's a happy cycle for love.

SPIRITUALITY
The Ring of Fire, the total solar eclipse on April 8, 2024, affects your sector of the higher mind. The eclipse will awaken fiery spiritual experiences. Incense, ritual fires, prayer candles and fire gazing are all techniques which might encourage spirituality. Travel to an area where the eclipse is visible to deepen your spirituality.

FINANCE
When Jupiter changes signs on May 26 better financial opportunities will manifest. The eclipse on March 13, 2025 is in your sector of earned income. A different source of cash flow or new employment is likely to be available then.

165

VIRGO
August 23–September 22
Spring 2024–Spring 2025 for those
born under the sign of the Virgin

Meticulous, caring, sensibly grounded and reasonable, this Mercury-ruled earth sign has a genuine gift for healing and problem solving. You are observant and always want to get everything organized. With good intentions and forever seeking perfection, Virgo is prone to be a worrier. Your wholesome dignity and considerate behavior will inspire the trust and admiration of coworkers and friends alike.

The Spring Equinox brings a Mars opposition to your Sun. This competitive aspect hints at some turbulence in a relationship. Dedicate a seasonal rite to compromise and harmony. Mercury will be retrograde in your 8th house April 1–25. An old mystery is solved. There can be some reshuffling of finances, especially regarding inherited or invested assets. By May Day Venus will trine your Sun. This soft and benevolent influence creates harmony in connections with in-laws as well as grandparent and grandchild interactions. Cultural events such art shows, concerts or theatrical productions can be enjoyable through May 23 while this trend is in force.

June begins with Jupiter crossing your midheaven. This influential transit affects your career sector. It will last through the end of the year. Opportunities to elevate your professional status can be available. Aspire. Have faith in yourself and try meeting a new challenge. You can definitely advance and grow. On June 9 Mars changes signs. Stress begins to lessen. A project is completed and there is time for a vacation. By the Summer Solstice you will feel closer to the land and nature.

During July your 11th house is highlighted. Plans involving a long-term goal are discussed. You will be aware of how influential associates can be. The New Moon on July 5 reveals specifics. By Lammas Mercury enters your 1st house. This heightens curiosity and sharpens your ability to process information. Honor the early harvest by sharing a poem or recipe at a seasonal gathering. August 5–28 Venus conjoins your Sun. Both business and social connections are promising. Express a creative idea. Make a beautiful presentation. The New Moon on September 2 brings a renewed sense of purpose and direction. As the Autumn Equinox nears a stimulating Mars aspect generates enthusiasm. Meetings and conversations from early September through Halloween provide you with the details needed to manifest a cherished dream. At Halloween a futuristic costume, perhaps inspired by a sci-fi story, would be a good choice.

The first half of November shifts your attention toward a family matter. A home repair project might be involved. Be a good listener, then you will know what steps to take by November 15. Throughout the last half of November an earthy Venus transit suggests appreciating nature. An outdoor stroll to take

166

scenic photos or to wildcraft some edible berries or nuts offers a diversion. At the New Moon on December 1 express gratitude in a meditation or ritual while looking ahead to the winter holiday season. Mars affects your 12th house at the Winter Solstice. An opportunity to help those in need is available. This could involve caring for an animal or assisting a vulnerable person. December 7–16 reveals the specifics. Surprise visitors interrupt plans but do provide congenial company December 17–31.

During January Venus highlights your section of partnerships. You will appreciate the accomplishments of someone close to you. A relationship with an especially intelligent or talented person warms your heart. Acknowledge a special achievement by dedicating a candle to this special someone on Candlemas, February 1–2. February 14–March 1 new points of view and different offers can encourage a change of direction. Information is shared which illuminates new options. A description of a situation is retold to reveal a different twist to a story after the Full Moon on March 5. As winter ends you will long to leave a situation which has grown stale. Open the windows and doors of your home to let a fresh March wind blow away winter's cobwebs on March 20, the last full day of winter.

HEALTH
This year you will sense changes in your health and vitality. The Total Lunar Eclipse in Virgo on March 4, 2025 brings valuable insights regarding your path to maintaining wellness. For self care develop your potential as an artist.

Blend some colors that express how you feel. Design a mandala incorporating words and symbols describing important milestones in your life. As a learning experience take time to appreciate everything that has touched your life, whether this has been for the good or not.

LOVE
Two Full Moons in a row this year, on June 21 and July 21, are unusual in that both lunations will fall in your 5th house of romance. This brings a unique opportunity either for a summer romance to nurture a new love or to rekindle happiness with a current partner. Plan to enjoy moon gazing with that special someone at those times. The moonbeams illuminate true love.

SPIRITUALITY
The Uranus retrograde from September 1 to January 30 affects your sector of philosophy and higher consciousness. This favors exploring past incarnations and accessing the Akashic Records, deepening spiritual awareness. This is also an excellent time to forgive. Releasing past traumas and anger helps with integrating spirituality.

FINANCE
Two of the eclipses this year, on March 25 and October 2, will be in your 2nd house of money. Expect the unexpected. A different source of income could replace the status quo. A favorable Jupiter influence from the Spring Equinox until May 24 brings promising financial potential. Examine options for enhancing financial security during that time.

167

LIBRA
September 23–October 23
Spring 2024–Spring 2025 for those
born under the sign of the Scales

Just as perfectly balanced Scales hint, this Venus-ruled sign is all about justice and equality. Called "a peaceful warrior," Libra is always ready to battle for what is right and fair. However, you prefer to avoid conflict. With compassion and gentleness you strive to maintain peace. Your quest involves artistry, balance and beauty in all things. Relationships of all kinds, business or personal, are at the core of what matters most to you. Vacillation can pose hurdles though. Finalizing decisions can be challenge.

The Spring Equinox finds Venus transiting your 6th house. This trend sets the pace until April 4. A loving animal companion offers solace and good company. You will make a special effort to maintain a peaceful, organized schedule. The March 25 lunar eclipse in Libra reveals important options and brings insights. A Mercury opposition which spans April through mid-May promises interesting and controversial conversations initiated by others. The last half of May accents your 8th house. This strengthens your interest in the spirit world and mysteries of the afterlife. Shop for vintage treasures. Visit an estate sale.

June 1–8 introduces a competitive situation. An opposition from Mars brings a dynamic person who can be quite assertive regarding key issues. During the remainder of June transits in your 9th house set the pace. You will long for wider horizons and could plan a long journey. Visiting sites of historical significance can pique your interest. At the Summer Solstice honor the longest of days by selecting an invocation or poem which draws upon the midsummer observances of another land. Saturn changes direction in your health sector at the end of June. Consider what choices are best regarding wellness. Diet and exercise are important factors. July introduces a strong focus on dreams and goals linked to your career. Guidance comes through the study of recent developments in your chosen field. Dedicate Lammas to long-term planning.

During August Venus creates a deep empathy with those who are vulnerable. There are concerns for situations which you feel should be remedied. The New Moon on September 2 allows you to release vague worries about any issues you can't affect. The lunar eclipse on September 17 brings a focus on developing a more efficient daily schedule and creating a more appealing work environment. Your connections with coworkers are changing. Someone new could become a part of your circle at work. At the Autumn Equinox the mood lightens. A sense of adventure and discovery prevails as your birthday approaches. The eclipse in Libra on October 2 brings insights regarding your personal growth process. There are choices to make. Finances improve during the 2nd and 3rd weeks of October. At Halloween you will especially enjoy fragrances.

168

Simmer a kettle of apple juice with a cinnamon stick. Add bay leaf, cloves and an orange peel. Use your artistic skill and carve a fabulous jack o' lantern. Save the seeds to toast.

From November 3 through early January your 3rd house is highlighted by Mercury. A variety of errands and plans will keep you very busy. Verify directions and details to keep things running smoothly while Mercury is retrograde November 25–December 15. Be flexible if loved ones are forgetful or confused. At the Winter Solstice Venus will be in your love and pleasure sector. Holiday gatherings will be especially merry and bright during the shortest of days. The Black Moon on December 30 accents your family traditions and ancestry.

Excitement and controversy colors your professional circle from January through the end of winter. Mars will be prominent in your 10th house of accomplishment and prominence. You can attract the attention of colleagues. Much is expected of you, but the extra effort you make propels you forward. At Candlemas light a golden taper to enhance status and success. Career progress comes your way after February 23. Venus turns retrograde in your relationship sector as March begins. One who was close to you in the past, perhaps an old flame, can return. Recall the past and you will understand the present and future.

HEALTH

Throughout the year Saturn and Neptune hover in your health sector. Patience in understanding and attending to health conditions will reward you with improved health. For self-care share an event with or plan a treat for a congenial friend. A suggestion would be to bake a cake or purchase tickets to see a film or concert together.

LOVE

The Full Moon on August 19 impacts your 5th house of love. Mutual attraction is encouraging near that time. During September Venus will transit Libra; this influence is very promising regarding love. When Venus goes retrograde March 1–April 15, 2025 keep it light and casual. Assume a wait and see approach to love. That time span isn't favorable for finalizing any kind of commitment.

SPIRITUALITY

Connecting with art and beauty encourages spiritual growth. Stroll through an art exhibit or purchase an arrangement of beautiful flowers to deepen your connection to spirituality. Sacred music and colors will heighten your connection with the divine. The eclipses in Libra on March 25, 2024 and October 2, 2024 awaken surprise twists in your spiritual path. This influence sparks spiritual growth.

FINANCE

Uranus will remain in Taurus, in your 8th house, all year. This can bring a monetary gift or a return on an investment to augment your earnings. From May 26 through the end of the winter Jupiter will trine your Sun. This benevolent aspect protects you from serious financial woes. Your essential needs will be covered.

SCORPIO
October 24–November 21
Spring 2024–Spring 2025 for those
born under the sign of the Scorpion

Free-spirited and sharp, the Scorpion weaves between order and chaos. Intense emotions and feelings are veiled by a reserved and dignified façade. Aware and conscious of truth you seek to understand the root causes of all that is known or unknown. The afterlife, the processes of birth and reincarnation always fascinate you. Pluto-ruled Scorpio endures and penetrates the unknown.

The Spring Equinox whispers in, arriving on wings of love as Venus brightens your sector of romance and pleasure through April 4. An upbeat Mars aspect follows, setting the pace April 5–29. Your energy and confidence will be high. Much is accomplished as a result. Near May Eve there is a subtle energy shift. Several planetary oppositions indicate controversy. Don't try to change anyone's opinion, just move forward maintaining independence. Live and let live. Wellness is a topic of study and conversation May 1–15 when Mercury highlights your health sector. Late May and early June shifts the focus to strengthening relationships. A sense of finality is evident at the New Moon on June 6. Jupiter and the Sun transit your 8th house dur-

ing mid-June, accenting endings and new beginnings.

At the Summer Solstice Venus and Mercury align with the Sun in your 9th house of adventure and higher consciousness. Travel, especially to a place of spiritual significance, can be on your agenda as summer begins. Visit a sacred place for ritual work and meditation on the longest of days. July ushers in a focus on your career sector. Your work will impress an influential person. A new position or project might be offered. Accept the challenge with enthusiasm. By Lammas your efforts meet with success. August 5–28 your 11th house is brightened by a Venus transit. This is favorable for deepening your involvement within an organization. Establish camaraderie. Your circle of friends is especially precious to you during August.

Early September ushers in a more introspective cycle. You will seek quiet reverie. The eclipse on September 17 brings creative inspiration and awakens new interests. At the Autumnal Equinox Venus crosses into Scorpio. This cycle of love and good cheer lasts through October 17. A social connection develops. Creative inspiration is present too. Write a poem or try an art project. Late October awakens new interests, Mercury will be strong so travel as well as lively discussions can be a focus. At Halloween a strong 2nd house makes you budget-conscious. A visit to a thrift store or yard sale brings vintage treasures to make into costumes or décor for the holiday season ahead.

By November 2 Mars begins a transit through your career sector. A competitive mood develops. Motivation is high. You will be inspired to do your best to achieve. professionally. The Full Moon on November 15 brings suggestions and inspiration from those close to you. Late November–December 15 finds Mercury retrograde in your finance sector. It's a good time to review your budget and expenses. A job or other source of income from the past could become available again. As the Winter Solstice nears decorate your home and plan a seasonal gathering. Venus brightens your sector of family and residence. Visitors and relatives are ready to celebrate. This happy trend prevails through January 2.

January finds Mars retrograde in your 9th house. This favors completing a course of study or finishing a manuscript which you started and then set aside in the past. The Full Moon on January 13 highlights the specifics. As February begins honor Candlemas with lights dedicated to healing. The emotional needs of a loved one pose a concern.

On February 4 Jupiter turns direct in your 8th house. A return on an investment or an inheritance adds to financial security. Your financial picture brightens throughout the rest of the winter. February 20–28 offers opportunities for pursuing a hobby or enjoying sports and games. March 1–20 brings favorable aspects from Mars, Saturn and the Sun. A milestone is achieved or a goal is reached at the lunar eclipse on March 14. Your energy level is high and much can be accomplished with ease as winter ends.

HEALTH

The very significant eclipse on April 8 affects your 6th house of health. There can be a breakthrough in overcoming any health challenges near that time. The eclipse favors considering new choices regarding healthcare. On October 11 Pluto, your ruler, completes its retrograde. This indicates improvement in your overall vitality. For self-care treat yourself to a ghost tour. Learn about validating and investigating paranormal phenomena.

LOVE

Saturn transits your love sector all year. A romantic interest who is a generation older or younger can capture your heart. You will seek stability, structure and loyalty within a relationship now. Late September through mid-October and January bring very promising Venus transits. Love can blossom then.

SPIRITUALITY

Time spent in quiet solitary reflection can be the catalyst for a spiritual awakening this year. The eclipses on March 25 and October 2 point to the weeks near the Vernal and Autumnal equinoxes as times to anticipate spiritual experiences. Prepare a seasonal altar to honor spiritual growth at spring and fall celebrations. A springtime or autumn walkabout could also provide the catalyst for a spiritual realization.

FINANCE

On May 26 Jupiter enters your 8th house where it remains through the end of the year while making a quincunx aspect to your Sun. Fate will affect your finances. Adapt to and analyze economic trends. An insurance settlement, return on an investment, an inheritance or gift can brighten your financial prospects.

171

SAGITTARIUS
November 22–December 20
Spring 2024–Spring 2025 for those
born under the sign of the Archer

Quick-witted, charming, competitive and philosophical, those born under the sign of the Centaur cherish freedom and stimulation. Your nature is that of a wanderer. Independence is so important to you that being confined to the same relationship or career for very long can quickly lose appeal. Animal companions are always dear to you.

The Vernal Equinox finds Venus in your sector of home and family, a trend which sets the pace through April 4. You will be motivated to improve your living circumstances. This might involve decorating or repairing your residence. Mercury is retrograde April 1–25 in your sector of wishes and social connections. There is uncertainty. Patiently gather information, then finalize plans. On May Day focus on nurturing friendships. During May a favorable Mars aspect enhances your energy and enthusiasm. Much can be accomplished. The Full Moon on May 23 in Sagittarius renews understanding and perspective.

During June Mars enters your 6th house. This is an excellent time to get organized. Develop an efficient daily schedule. At the Summer Solstice, the longest of days, prepare a feast, perhaps a picnic, of seasonal fruits and fresh bread. Dedicate an observance or affirmation to wellness of both mind and body. July begins with Saturn retrograde in your 4th house. A family member seeks emotional support and understanding. Diffuse a bit of emotional drama kindly with humor. July 2–25 a favorable Mercury aspect promises productive travel as well as an interest in learning something new. July favors making choices regarding career aspirations.

On Lammas affirm peace and harmony. A Mars opposition affects the entire month of August. Compromise to diffuse an impending conflict just after the New Moon on August 4. September begins with a harmonious Venus sextile. A caring and talented friend supports your dreams and goals. This is an optimal time for getting more involved with an interesting club or organization. Team efforts are fulfilling. The eclipse on September 17 brings the needs of relatives into focus. A family member might share a surprise announcement. As Summer melds into autumn changes for the better are developing.

October 1–8 Sun and Mercury placements support the manifestation of a long cherished wish. Travel, imported items and community service can be a focus. On October 9 Jupiter, your ruler, begins a retrograde cycle. This impacts your 7th house of partnerships until early February. Someone who was very close to you in the past returns and a behavior pattern repeats. By October 18 Venus brings a positive and promising mood which lasts through November 11. Accept or send invitations, plan or attend a party. Social prospects; including love connections, are promising. Assemble a glamorous or celebrity look-alike costume for Halloween. Late October to mid-November is a splendid time to express creative ideas and enjoy the arts.

Mercury begins a long transit through your birth sign in November which lasts until January 7. Lively conversations, the exchange of ideas and a series of short journeys will set the pace during this entire time. The New Moon on December 1 in Sagittarius offers insights and enlightenment. An old grudge or misunderstanding can be released then. At the Winter Solstice celebrate with seasonal songs, festive stories and poetry. January 8–20 your financial sector is highlighted by both the Sun and Mercury. Thoughts and conversations will involve earning power and cash flow then. A new source of income becomes available. A business meeting is productive near the Full Moon on January 13.

From late January through the end of Winter Mars highlights your 8th house of mystery and the afterlife. At Candlemas dedicate an altar to honor those who have passed on. A caring spirit visits from the afterlife with messages expressing love and concern.

Be conscientious and attend to details at work during February. A strong Saturn influence then promises that extra effort and patience in completing career obligations will be appreciated by influential colleagues. The specifics are clarified near the eclipse on March 14, 2025. In March Venus turns retrograde. This indicates karmic or past life influences in love. For the time being keep your relationship status as is though. Considerate behavior and good manners will smooth the way in all kinds of relationships during March.

HEALTH
From late May through the end of the Winter control excesses of all kinds, from extreme sports to choices in food and drink. For self-care take time to learn something new. Explore new intellectual challenges. Check out documentaries featuring travel to places with an intriguing history.

LOVE
The total solar eclipse on April 8 has a profound impact on your love sector. A new romantic connection can blossom then or an existing relationship may deepen to a new level of intimacy. You often will begin and end relationships abruptly. Try gently developing a love connection gradually this year. April and October 18–November 11 are promising love cycles.

SPIRITUALITY
Rapport with animal companions is always an important part of your spiritual development. Psychic connections with either domestic animals or wild creatures can provide especially deep spiritual experiences. Explore Native American studies for meeting spirit animal guides. The Full Moon on November 15 can open spiritual awareness.

FINANCE
Always try to enjoy what you have rather than lamenting what you might lack when it comes to finances. Finances take a promising turn late in the Winter after Jupiter goes direct on February 4. Saturn's influence this year rewards sustained effort and patience with solid profits.

CAPRICORN
December 22–January 19
Spring 2024–Spring 2025 for those
born under the sign of the Goat

The dedicated and punctual Goat approaches life as a serious business. Grounding and building are the priorities of this Saturn-ruled earth sign. You are loyal and well organized. You do have a sly and humorous side too. Only those fortunate enough to know you well get to share in the light-hearted irony which characterizes your real outlook on life.

The Vernal Equinox finds Mars exiting your money sector. You are catching up with expenses and budgeting. Greet the season to come with prosperity affirmations. The eclipse on March 25 brings changes in your career path. Adapt to new trends to assure success. During April several transits affect your sector of home and heritage. There can be some surprising choices expressed by relatives. A home renovation project or move might be considered following the great eclipse on April 8. By May Day favorable 5th house transits affect your sector of love and pleasure. Vacation plans or other enjoyable recreational activities brighten the first three weeks of May.

June brings a focus on wholesome foods and lifestyle choices. Your vitality improves at the New Moon on June 6. The remainder of June brings you pleasure through the accomplishments of those who are close to you. A legal issue is resolved favorably near the Summer Solstice. Include a purple candle for justice on your Solstice altar. On June 21 honor the Full Moon in Capricorn. A cherished wish is fulfilled. On June 29 Saturn turns retrograde in your 3rd house. A cycle begins which finds you analyzing current events and patiently sifting through communication which comes your way. The effort to clarify information and get the facts continues as a background theme in your life through mid-November. During the first part of July Mars favorably aspects your Sun. Your energy level and enthusiasm brighten. You will be motivated to take on new challenges. An exercise program or sports can be especially beneficial July 1–19.

As Lammas nears you will focus on managing investments and other financial considerations. Research brings valuable insights. August through early September brings an interest in studying the deeper meaning of life. Meditation sessions can enhance your connections with spirit guardians or angels. The New Moon on September 2 brings understanding through nuances and hunches. On September 5 Mars moves into an opposition to your Sun. Your 7th house is affected. This competitive energy continues through the Winter. Focus on cooperation. Cultivate a spirit of camaraderie and nurture team players. At the Autumnal Equinox celebrate inclusiveness.

October 1–12 a Mercury influence stirs your 10th house. Multitasking complicates your days. Prioritize. Make time to relax. Release stress. Late October accents new dreams and goals. By

Halloween you will realize that you have outgrown the past. Welcome a new range of possibilities. A Halloween costume which creates suspense and mystery would be ideal. Think of a mysterious wanderer; the Tarot's Hermit, swirled in a cloak carrying a walking stick.

November 12–December 5 Venus glides through Capricorn activating your 1st house. Your charisma is at a peak. Others will be attracted to you. Invitations arrive. During the last three weeks of December a Mars retrograde influence affects your 8th house. Afterlife connections arise. Honor the memory of lost loved ones. At the Winter Solstice the warmth of candlelight or firelight heals your thoughts and eases poignant recollections. At the New Moon on December 30 release the past. Embrace the future.

January favors travel. Mercury is in your birth sign. This assures a quick wit and skillful communication. In early February a strong Mars aspect brings dynamic people into your life. Someone close to you makes plans or offers suggestions. At Candlemas analyze how others are affecting you. Light an empowerment candle if you sense your confidence wavering. March begins with Venus turning retrograde in your sector of home and heritage. Past habit patterns and inherited characteristics can affect family dynamics. A visit from a long-lost relative or old friend is likely near the end of Winter.

HEALTH

Jupiter transits your 6th house of health from May 26 through the rest of the Winter. This is very promising for healing of any health concerns and for maintaining wellness. Jupiter does represent expansion though, so be sure to maintain a healthy weight. Especially avoid high calorie goodies while Jupiter is retrograde October 9–February 4. Self-care for you is linked with keeping to a well developed daily plan which keeps you from wasting valuable time and resources. Vary the routine with each season though to keep the day's pace from becoming the daily grind.

LOVE

Building a solid base, a secure future together would be a part of your ideal relationship. Mars transits your 7th house of partnerships from early September through November 2 and again January 5–March 19. During those times you will be inclined to nurture a meaningful commitment or end a situation which just isn't meant to be.

SPIRITUALITY

Your spirituality sector is influenced by Mercury. Travel to sacred sites and literature about spiritual topics will awaken your spiritual inclinations. The total lunar eclipse of March 14, 2025 has profound spiritual implications for you. Plan to attend a drum circle, moon ritual or other spiritual activity at that time.

FINANCE

During most of May earth sign transits will favorably aspect your Sun. May favors prosperity and abundance. Two eclipses this year do affect your 10th house of career success though. Flexibility, staying in tune with changing dynamics regarding your profession, is important in sustaining your financial security.

AQUARIUS
January 20–February 18
Spring 2024–Spring 2025 for those
born under the sign of the Water Bearer

As the ultimate humanitarians, Aquarians delight in relieving the heartaches and disappointments of others. Friendships are cherished, yet you have an independent side which inclines toward detachment if an association grows too dependent. With a touch of eccentricity you have a desire to rattle the status quo and make changes. Your originality makes you seem both intriguing and perplexing, and you are always memorable.

At the Vernal Equinox Mars is in your birth sign. You long to challenge situations which are less than satisfactory. By March 23 this trend softens and there is a shift in focus. Your 2nd house is highlighted by Venus as April begins. A friend suggests a new source of income. Your artistry adds to your earning potential. During the last part of April your sector of neighbors and siblings is active. A neighborhood meeting or social event strengthens your circle of acquaintances. A relative shares significant news near May Day. Be a good listener. May 1–23 Venus joins Jupiter and Uranus in your 4th house. A home renovation or decorating idea has appeal. You will feel a renewed connection to your heritage and could discover an interesting family anecdote from long ago.

From the end of May to mid-June Venus trines your Sun. A relationship becomes more intimate and love blossoms near the New Moon on June 6. A favorite leisure time activity, perhaps including a sport or game, brightens the days leading up to the Summer Solstice. Celebrate the longest of days with loved ones.

July brings an urge to get organized. Consider ways to make your work space more comfortable. As Lammas approaches others make plans which affect you. Your cooperation will be appreciated and rewarded. Mercury will be retrograde during most of August. Insights into past lives are likely. Understanding a karmic connection with someone whom you've known in another incarnation comes in a dream or meditation near the time of the Full Moon on August 19.

As August ends a business meeting emphasizes loyalty and teamwork. September 1–22 finds Venus affecting your 9th house. Imported items will appeal to you. Try the recipes, listen to the music or learn a few phrases in the language of another land. Uranus, your ruler, begins a retrograde cycle on September 1. Expect a dejavu if visiting an unfamiliar destination. A journey abroad would be inspirational and enjoyable. At the Autumnal Equinox Venus crosses your midheaven. This relates to status and reputation. Put on the charm to make a lasting good impression. Place a mirror on your altar to help in visualizing your higher self as you welcome the new season.

October 1–12 a favorable Mercury influence supports learning experiences. Attend a class or read a newly released book to widen your perspectives. Conversations will be revealing and stimulating during the remainder of October. Get others talking. Ask questions. At Halloween start a conversation about ritual observances or discuss costumes. By November 4 Mars enters your 7th house where it will remain throughout the winter holiday season. Happiness in a close partnership will become a priority. Tolerance and humor help. Pursue shared goals to deepen an important bond with someone who is important to you. Celebrate a commitment at the Winter Solstice. Toast each other with champagne, hot cocoa or wassail on the longest of nights.

During January Venus enters your financial sector where it will join both Saturn and Neptune. This can bring extra money your way, yet you might worry about finances. Focus on enjoying all you have and have faith. Somehow it might be difficult to accurately assess money matters. Avoid being overly generous with others. Offer encouragement and helpful suggestions instead of giving more than you can spare. At Candlemas prepare prosperity candles and affirmations. February 1–13 a strong Mercury transit brings a burst of mental energy. Solutions come while you're considering options and gathering information. The last half of February finds Mars turning direct in your 6th house. Animal companions offer love and comfort. A new pet can find its way into your home and heart. March finds both Venus and Mercury going retrograde in your sector of transportation and communication. A new vehicle or alternative method of getting around can be needed. You will be curious and may explore new pathways and routes. A friend or relative who has been absent reconnects with you near the lunar eclipse on March 14.

HEALTH
Be gentle with yourself if involved in a demanding fitness program or extreme sports this year. Always focus on keeping comfortable when temperatures are extreme. You need warmth during the cold winter and to stay cool during the hot summer. For self-care getting involved with volunteer positions can bring rewarding experiences. Try making snacks for the needy, tutoring school children, caring for animals in need or visiting patients in care facilities.

LOVE
Your most successful relationships will usually begin by establishing a firm foundation of friendship. Venus, the cosmic love goddess, will be favorable during the first half of June and again in December. True love can be successfully nurtured during those times.

SPIRITUALITY
The eclipses on March 25 and October 2 both impact your 9th house of travel and higher consciousness. Visiting a sacred site or spiritual group near those times can facilitate a significant spiritual awakening.

FINANCE
Patience and persistence are your keynotes this year regarding finance. Serious Saturn transits your sector of money matters. The challenge is to live within your means, enjoy what you have and develop a financial strategy; then the money will flow freely.

PISCES
February 19–March 20
Spring 2024–Spring 2025 for those
born under the sign of the Fish

Those born under the sign of the Fish are imaginative and serene individuals who long to be allowed to live in a peaceful dream world. It's important for you to find a constructive creative outlet. Avoid being drawn into escapism. Set aside time each day for meditation, solitude or artistic pursuits. Strolling along the beach or dancing to soothing music can be appealing. Yours is a gentle nature. You gravitate toward mystical and spiritual interests with the goal of developing your intuition and a deeper rapport with the sacred side of life.

From the Vernal Equinox though April 4 Venus glides though Pisces. You will be admired and appreciated; others are charmed by you. Both social and business connections can be productive. Throughout the remainder of April much can be accomplished. Mars is in your 1st house. You will be more assertive than usual. Focus on creative work or self improvement projects. May 1–15 affects your money sector. Thoughts and conversations will revolve around your income and spending power. May Day finds you planning a shopping spree in order to purchase gifts or a long desired personal item. Late May to mid-June will focus on family-oriented activities and

making home improvements. Visitors arrive near the Summer Solstice. On the shortest of nights a patio or yard party, perhaps featuring a gathering around a bonfire for a sing-along, would be a great way to welcome summer vacation. Neptune, your ruler, begins a retrograde cycle on July 2. This strikes a nostalgic note. You can enjoy reunions and reminiscing during the weeks preceding Lammas. Near the Full Moon on July 21 a dream resurrects past life recollections.

During August Mercury and Venus emphasize your sector of partnerships. You will give considerable thought to the future of an important commitment. You are proud of the accomplishments of someone close to you. Early September brings improvements in finances. A return on an investment or other payment arrives. The eclipse on September 17 in Pisces brings changes in the status quo. By the Autumnal Equinox the specifics are revealed. Prepare a gratitude altar and give thanks for new opportunities. A change for the better in your residence or career path might be appear on the horizon. September 23–October 17 Venus will favorably influence your 9th house. A relationship with a grandparent or grandchild is especially enjoyable. This is a good cycle for travel too. You would enjoy exploring a faraway place and learning about another culture. At Halloween share photos and memories of your journeys and adventures. The art and folklore of a destination you visited can inspire you to try a foreign twist as a costume idea. On November 4 Mars begins a transit through your health sector. Seek ways to alleviate stress and

178

ease your workload. This dynamic cycle lasts through the winter. It's a time to be gentle with yourself. Exercise moderately and get enough rest.

December brings progress involving your career. Communicate with colleagues to enhance success. After December 16 situations are more settled. By the Winter Solstice you will experience progress. Bless your work space with sage and salt on the shortest of days to disperse discordant energies. On January 3 Venus enters Pisces where it will remain through Candlemas. Add beauty to yourself and your surroundings. It's a good time to try arts and crafts projects or attend a play or concert. Spruce up your wardrobe and décor. Early February brings a desire for privacy. At Candlemas light a blue candle dedicated to insulate against those who drain your energy. The mood changes when Mercury transits your sign February 14–March 2. You will find communication stimulating and inspirational. Accept invitations in late February, especially if a short jaunt is involved.

Review your budget early in March. Retrograde transits in your money sector at that time hint that you might have high monthly bills. Seek ways to conserve resources. The eclipse on March 14 affects your 7th house of close partnerships. As the winter ends an association is evolving and changing. Make the best of this by making an effort to understand the other person's point of view and needs.

HEALTH
Saturn remains in Pisces all year. Patience is important regarding health care. The health consequences of past lifestyle choices, for good or not, will be apparent. So will hereditary factors. For self-care focus on the health of your feet. Feet can affect your overall wellness. Reflexology, comfortable shoes and foot baths with Epsom salts or healing herbs can be rejuvenating.

LOVE
Mars, the planet of passion, will pass through your 5th house of romance September 5–November 3 and again from January 6 through the end of winter. This promises an epic love connection. It's likely to be stormy and tempestuous rather than sweet and serene. The Full Moon on January 13 brings a hint concerning details.

SPIRITUALITY
Neptune, the indicator of spirituality, will transit Pisces all year. You are evolving spiritually. Dream interpretation can be useful for understanding your spiritual path. While Neptune is retrograde July 2–December 7 past life regression can be helpful. Consider traveling to visit the scene of an important past life recollection.

FINANCE
The eclipses on March 25 and October 2 affect your 8th house. This can indicate income from an investment, settlement or partnership. The eclipse on April 8 impacts your 2nd house of earned income. This whole pattern points to surprises involving finances. Be receptive to new financial strategies. Avoid lending or borrowing money

Sites of Awe

The Rhine River

Today I have the pleasure of taking a cruise down Germany's Rhine River. I'm very excited about this. I really can't wait to see the Lorelei, a large rock located in an area of the river that becomes narrow and bends around a sharp corner. I need to be patient—I believe we will be cruising down the river for a couple of hours before we reach it.

According to one legend, the Lorelei was once a beautiful young maiden who lived on the cliff above the Rhine River. She was so beautiful that sailors would become distracted and crash their boats on the rocks below. Some versions of the legend say that the maiden was actually a siren or water spirit who used her singing to lure sailors to their doom. I'm just hoping to hear her song!

We have a good day—the sun is shining but it isn't too warm. The boat is nice-looking and it can carry over 200 people on the day cruise. Well, getting on the boat now and as I hand my ticket to the man on the dock, I notice that he is dressed in old-world traditional garb. I'm sure it is meant to please the tourists but I prefer to think of his attire as something to get me prepared to "see" what is hidden from most folks who travel down the river. I'm also hoping to feel the energy of the sites we pass and hear the mysterious sounds of the water spirits. Lots of wishful thinking going on here.

Throughout history the Rhine has played a significant role in shaping the culture and mythology of the people who live along its banks. Because the Rhine was home to Celtic and German peoples,

Lorelei figure overlooking the Rhine

180

Kaub town and medieval castle Gutenfels

the river is rich in legends, myths and folklore that date back centuries. Oh, I better stop drifting into nostalgia and find a seat. I'll pick something on the shady side. I'm not fond of the hot sun.

Well, now that they are done with the infernal announcements, we can get started. Immediately I can see that this is wine country. There are vineyards on both sides of the banks. I remember that many years ago our Coven used to use a red German wine at ritual and it is fun to think that it might have come from here. I think I will check out the inside cabin to see if they serve wine…and they do! A glass of Rhine white to kick off the tour sounds awesome. Oh, it is sweeter than I thought. I have always preferred red wine, but as they say "When in Rome…"

Heading back outside. I don't want to miss anything.

The tall banks on both sides come down to rows of small quaint homes and other buildings. Here they meet the river. As the voyage continues, I see castles on both sides. They are high up on the hills. From their vantage point, observers could see up and down the Rhine for miles. And these castles are architecturally magnificent! There is power exuding from them as if they were dragons perched on the hilltops. The towers reach to the clouds as if pointing or calling down power or lightning. They are absolutely breathtaking. There is a majesty about these giants on the hills— they seem to have authority to defend or to defeat. Either way, the sense of power is prevalent. Every castle seems to have its homes, village and church residing in its shadow. This structure of the society reminds me of the structures in nature. In medieval times, people lived closer to the land and therefore there was a symbiotic mimicry between the two. Today we live according to efficiency and profit, leaving the natural laws behind, and little knowing how much power we leave behind with them.

Going inside again because it is time for another glass of wine. That first one went down very easily. The bartender

181

Medieval Heidelberg

is suggesting a different wine—still a white. I'll try that. Ah, less sweet, and very delicious. Better take a picture of the bottle for later.

Oh, there are cable cars in the vineyards on the side of the mountain. Don't know what I was expecting but I guess cable cars are an easier way to travel up these steep hills.

Our multi-storied boat offers a great view of both sides of the river. On one side, there is a rail line that hugs the river. I'm assuming that it goes the entire distance since some of the tours start hundreds of miles up the river. I think that tours must go in both directions with passengers taking the train back to their starting point.

Time for another glass of wine.

While I am in here, I can see a large dining room onboard. I'll come back here for a snack before too long. Back outside!

I've been waiting to hear something about the local folklore but the staff isn't saying much. Everyone is busy but I did find some pamphlets and reading material at the side of the bar. This one says that:

The Rhine river has a rich occult and metaphysical significance that has been preserved through the ages. The Celts believed that the river was a sacred place and home to spirits and gods. The Romans also saw the river as a place of divine significance, and many temples were built along its banks. The Rhine also has a rich history in alchemy and magic. The river's water was said to have healing properties, and many alchemists used it in their experiments. The famous alchemist Paracelsus believed that the Rhine river was the source of the philosopher's stone, a substance that could turn base metals into gold and give eternal life. The philosopher's stone was believed to be hidden somewhere along the Rhine, and many alchemists searched for it along the river's banks.

I also remember reading that Aleister Crowley claimed to be initiated into the

182

Golden Dawn by the spirit of the Rhine. Crowley was said to see the Rhine as a place of power and he used its energy in his rituals.

My, this is a nice excursion. The weather is just beautiful and I am enjoying the information in these brochures. This one says that,

The Rhine river has been the source of many myths and legends throughout history. The ancient Celts believed that the river was the home of the goddess of the Rhine, who was the protector of the river and its people. The goddess was said to have the power to control the river's currents and protect the people from danger.

Nice!

Well, I think it is time for a snack. This dining area is fairly large but very few folks are in here. Perfect time to avoid lines. Interesting menu but I don't eat meat and most of the options have sausage. Hum. After asking about a vegetarian option, spätzle was suggested. I'll try it.

Gazing out the window, I've almost drifted off for a nap but my server woke me with the spätzle. Wow, this is like mac' and cheese but much better! It might be better tasting but I'm sure the atmosphere has a lot to do with it. I need to wolf this down, get a glass of wine and get back outside to see what is next. I'm hoping to see or hear one of the Rhine Maidens, the three beautiful mermaids who lived in the depths of the river and were said to guard the Rhine's treasure—a vast hoard of gold!

Along this river, passing from Switzerland through Germany and

The legendary Loreley Rock at the river Rhine

183

the Netherlands before reaching the North Sea, the folklore is rich. And much of it concerns the Lorelei— this steep, rocky cliff rises over four hundred feet above the eastern bank of the Rhine. The name "Lorelei" means "murmuring rock" in German. The Lorelei is one of the most famous and significant landmarks on the river and for a great many years it has been associated with mystical and supernatural powers.

Oh dear, someone is coming around with a tray of complimentary wine. Ok... just one more glass.

I'm asking this very nice woman with the tray of wine about the Lorelei and she says that it is coming up in just a few minutes. I'm headed to the front left side of the boat to get a good view. Camera loaded, everything ready, wine in hand, I'm all set...

And, there it is! People are rushing to the side of the boat to take pictures. After taking a few, I'm just going to stand here and see with my "magic eyes" and listen with my "magic ears" to see if I can sense her—the siren!

I hear a song. Don't know where it is coming from but my eyes are shut and I don't want to open them. It sounds as if it is coming from off in the distance but from all directions at once. A soft melody, tempting, seductive and alluring. The hair on the back of my neck is standing at attention. I need time to listen...

Words fail me when trying to give more details about the song. I think it is one continuous song but I'm not sure. It almost gives me the sense of going into Fairy—like a "betwixt"

sound not of human making. Although I would not say that the sound makes me emotional, the experience certainly does. I'm so very glad to be blessed by the spirit of water.

As we pass the bend in the river and continue down the Rhine, the song is fading off in the distance but a new song has begun as a four-piece German brass band begins playing Die Lorelei. I'm wondering how long folks have been visiting here to witness the large rock that has held its mystery for so many years. I'm so grateful for this cherished visit and look forward to the time when I can bring others here on this river journey to visit the siren of legend.

Afterthoughts:

In more recent times, the Lorelei has been associated with various occult movements and secret societies. Some believe that the cliff is a portal to other dimensions or that it has some kind of mystical power that can be harnessed for magical purposes. Others believe that the Lorelei is connected to the ley lines that crisscross the Earth and that it has a special role in the spiritual energy of the planet.

The occult significance of the Lorelei is also reflected in the works of many famous writers and artists. For example, the German writer Heinrich Heine wrote a poem about the Lorelei in which he described the siren's enchanting singing voice and the danger it posed to sailors. The poem has been set to music by many composers—including Franz Liszt and Friedrich Silcher—and it is still popular today.

—ARMAND TABER

184

Odin's Ravens

ODIN'S RAVENS are an integral part of Norse mythology and are closely tied to the God's insight and influence over Fate. Depicted as intelligent, powerful and mysterious, they play a significant role in the stories and legends of Norse mythology. Called the Wanderer, the Deceiver and the Blind Guest, Odin is the chief god of the Aesir, a group of Gods and Goddesses from the North who reside in the realm of Asgard. Odin is known for his wisdom, magic and prowess in battle and he is often depicted with two ravens at his side. Named Huginn and Muninn, these ravens are said to be the Slain God's eyes and ears and they play a significant role in his stories.

Huginn's name means "thought" and embodies Odin's wit and cunning. Muninn's name means "memory" and embodies Odin's recollections over the many generations of his long reign over the Gods. Together the ravens represent the knowledge and wisdom of the Masked One and are a symbol of his power and influence. In legend, Huginn and Muninn are Odin's faithful companions and they are often depicted perched on his shoulders or flying over his head. Intelligent and wise, the ravens serve as Odin's scouts, gathering information and bringing it back to him. In some stories they even have the ability to shape shift into human form!

In Norse mythology ravens are associated with death and the afterlife. Their function as carrion birds tied them closely to the Lord of the Hanged—they consumed the bodies of sacrificed victims hung in the sacred grove outside Uppsala and presumably did so at other sacred sites as well. Ravens are also said to be present at the death of warriors along with the Valkyries who gather the souls of the fallen and carry them to Valhalla—Odin's hall of the slain where heroic warriors live on after death.

The Allfather is a God of wisdom and magic who is able to see and shape the future and in Norse mythology his ravens are closely tied to Fate as well. Said to be able to see into the future themselves, Huginn and Muninn are able to influence events just like the God they serve.

185

Reviews

The Grimoire Encyclopaedia: Volumes 1 & 2: A convocation of spirits, texts, materials, and practices
David Rankine
Vol 1: ISBN-13: 978-1914166365
Vol 2: ISBN-13: 978-1914166372
Hadean Press Limited
$44.99 each

FROM TIME TO TIME, an author undertakes an intellectual odyssey into the profound domains of esoteric wisdom, diligently documenting their expedition as they traverse uncharted territories. Reserve a spot on your bookshelves, for David Rankine has symbolically ascended the peak of Mount Sinai, reemerging with two paramount volumes that are an absolute necessity for any magician's library. Within the pages of Volume 1 and Volume 2 of *Encyclopaedia: Volumes 1 & 2: A convocation of spirits, texts, materials, and practices* an invaluable assemblage of summaries along with an examination of magical beings awaits, spanning 756 and 676 pages respectively. These volumes contain an abundance of indispensable knowledge that will leave no aspiring magician wanting.

In Volume 1, Rankine commences with a succession of concise lectures that serve as a guiding light for both novice journeymen and seasoned travelers along the mystical path. In the initial exposition, he indulges the reader with a swift exploration of the pre-grimoire era, meticulously noting the origins and sources of this arcane knowledge. This significant segment of the book also encompasses a profound treatise on the enigmatic "Spirit Hierarchies," a subject seldom addressed in other literary works of this nature. Another noteworthy gem presents itself in the form of an extensive analysis on the intricate art of "Conjuration." Rankine delves deep into the realms of conjuration, leaving no stone unturned as he explores ritualistic modes and methodologies. Concluding this section, he graciously provides a comprehensive timeline of texts, granting readers a glimpse into the evolutionary journey of the grimoire tradition through time.

Having established a firm foundation for the reader, Rankine proceeds to embark on the expansive domain of the "Encyclopedic Entries" section, which fills the remaining 756 pages. It is within these pages that the brilliance of this invaluable tome truly shines. For each entry, Rankine meticulously provides key details such as the estimated date of the text, the language in which it is written, the primary influences that shaped its composition, the origin of the book itself, the location of the maximum segment size (MSS) and whether the ritual employs a Circle as its modus operandi. Additionally, he includes a comprehensive list of tools utilized and an array of spirits associated with each text, accompanied by a concise yet highly informative description. Concluding each entry, Rankine offers an overview of essential readings, guiding readers towards further exploration and study.

Volume 2 presents a compilation of appendices meticulously curated by Rankine, delving into the diverse aspects of the rituals elucidated within the manuscripts featured in Volume 1. These appendices serve as a valuable reference, cross-referencing the manuscripts to provide deeper insights. For instance, in Appendix II, Rankine provides a comprehensive inventory of incense ingredients, encompassing details such as the specific type of incense, its form when employed, its purpose, planetary attributions and the texts in which it is mentioned. Beyond cataloging the ritualistic elements, Rankine goes the extra mile by documenting various modalities, including the utilization of magical circles and other pertinent practices. These appendices enrich the reader's understanding and offer a comprehensive resource for further exploration.

Only a handful of books can be classified as unequivocal essentials for any magical library. *The Grimoire Encyclopaedia: Volumes 1 & 2: A convocation of spirits, texts, materials, and practices* is not a mere collection that you read once and allow to accumulate dust on your shelf. Instead, it is a set that will inevitably bear the marks of frequent use, reflecting its indispensability.

Bending the Binary; Polarity Magic in a Nonbinary World
Deborah Lipp
ISBN-13: 978-0738772622
Llewellyn Publications
$18.99

TOPICS TOUCHING ON social issues tend to be divisive, and polarity is no exception. But where many magical communities have drawn firm battle lines, Lipp refuses to do so. *Bending the Binary* explores the history and practical applications of polarity as an occult principle and magical technology from a position of many years of experience and from a deep love of magic, magical traditions and magical people. Treating polarity neither as disposable and oppressive nor as immovable, essential and irrevocably tied to the sexual characteristics of the physical body, Lipp outlines its broad role in occultism and its application in modern magical traditions, especially as it pertains to magical partnership. Keeping one eye always on the practical, she includes numerous exercises for readers wishing to explore polarity more deeply in their own practices. She also suggests journal and discussion prompts at various points throughout the book to allow readers to personally engage with the complex and potentially challenging ideas she presents.

In addition to its refusal to engage in polemic, there are two primary features that separate this book from the numerous blog articles on the subject and the few other books that discuss magical polarity from a queer perspective. First is its deep dive into the history of polarity in the occult, discussing its role in Kabbalism, alchemy and other older forms of occultism in addition to its post-Golden Dawn interpretations and its use in Wiccan traditions. Second— and perhaps most important—is that it is rooted in the author's own story and the evolution of her own magical practices over time. She discusses how she was trained as a Witch in relation to polarity and the ways in which she both upholds and adapts that training within her majority-queer coven.

Not everything that comes to you from the past is a treasure, but not everything old is obsolete, either. Occult traditions come to the present through a gilt-framed Victorian filter, which does not always make them appear to match very well with many occultists' modern lives. Lipp presents the possibility that you can accept, use and even love that frame without feeling that you need to redecorate your whole house to match it.

Liber Kaos
Peter Carroll
ISBN-13: 978-1578638048
Weiser Books
$18.95

Chaos Magic, also known as Kaos Magic—has gained popularity in recent decades. Peter J. Carroll, a key figure in its formalization and popu-

larization, has made significant contributions to the tradition. His three foundational books, published closely together, shaped the Chaos Magic movement in the early 2000s.

The new edition of *Liber Kaos*, released thirty years after its original publication, is a valuable resource for chaos magic practitioners. Carroll's updates and additions provide insightful perspectives and enhancements.

Liber Kaos serves as a comprehensive guide to chaos magic, explaining its core principles and practical applications. Carroll's writing style is clear, engaging and accessible to beginners and experienced practitioners alike. He adeptly communicates complex ideas with precision and clarity.

This edition stands out for its additional material, expanding on the original content. Carroll's own experiences and evolving thoughts bring fresh insights to the book. His continued presence in the Chaos Magic community remains significant.

The book covers various topics, including the theory and history of magic, practical rituals, and exercises. Carroll skillfully blends psychology, quantum physics and traditional occultism, creating a powerful and unique magical system. Readers will explore sigil magic, astral travel, invocation, divination and more, gaining a comprehensive toolkit for their magical journeys.

Liber Kaos distinguishes itself by promoting personal experimentation and creativity within the chaos magic framework. Carroll encourages readers to develop their own methods,

188

adapt existing techniques and explore new approaches. This empowers individuals to customize their magical paths according to their specific needs and aspirations.

The inclusion of practical exercises, rituals and examples throughout the book enhances readers' understanding and application of the material. The step-by-step instructions and perceptive explanations enable both novice and advanced magicians to embark on their magical experiments with confidence.

Star Magic
Sandra Kynes
ISBN-13: 978-1-959883-00-5
Crossed Crow Books
$26.95

"...the dust of whose feet are the hosts of heaven..." The stars are a source of awe and inspiration for Witches and Pagans alike, but how many gaze in wonder at the night sky but have few resources aside from Astrology for engaging with the stars spiritually or working with them magically? In a revised and updated edition from Crossed Crow Books, *Star Magic* by Sandra Kynes offers a guide to the stars and constellations beyond the Zodiac.

Kynes begins with an overview of how stars were used in magic historically and then moves quickly to removing the practical barriers that keep many readers from working with the stars. She provides information on reading star maps as well as how best to use apps that provide similar information to traditional star maps.

Combined with the appendix that lists the latitudes of major cities worldwide, readers will be furnished with the tools and information to find any constellation or star they choose to view in the night sky. She moves on to guiding the reader in doing energy work with the stars before delving into the heart of the book, which is the detailed information about each constellation.

Organized seasonally, four chapters focus on the stars visible from the Northern Hemisphere in Spring, Summer, Winter and Fall, with an additional chapter on the Southern Hemisphere. Within each entry, Kynes provides the mythology and history of each constellation as well as significant stars within the constellation, the abbreviations used on star maps, information about each star's meaning, magical uses and ritual suggestions for connecting with the energy of that star or constellation spiritually and magically. She includes several useful appendices in addition to the latitudes of cities—tables of star colors for use in color magic, information on the fixed stars of Medieval magic (Agrippa's Behenian stars,) and dates of meteor showers.

Whether you live in the country and stand in wonder at the night sky regularly or you live in the city and hope to connect with the energy of the constellations beyond what light pollution allows you to see, with Kynes' wealth of knowledge and practical guidance, you will be well equipped to turn your star gazing into star magic.

From a Witch's Mailbox

This house is now clean

Should I cleanse my home before I do magic rituals and can you suggest a method?—Submitted by Carey Kraus

Well that really depends on a few variables. As a practitioner of magic you might want to establish a regimen of magical hygiene. At a very basic level, as a magician or Witch you become a sort of beacon for all kinds of entities that can either help or hinder your magical endeavors. Further to this point, these energies don't necessarily distinguish between your mundane or magical life. As for suggestion, there are numerous ways of cleansing your home. For a quick fix, a fumigation with frankincense and myrrh will do in a pinch. This would be the case for magician and Wiccan alike. On a more meta level, you would do well to make a habit of a big cleansing once a month and quick fumigation reinforcement when a need arises. On a monthly basis, each entrance into your home (windows included) should get an asperging with salt water, the floor of each room should be cleansed with a wash (salt water, water with a small amount of ammonia or perfumed water are good choices) and each room should be fumigated with a purificatory incense of your choice—frankincense, myrrh, juniper or sage are good choices. There certainly are other methods that also

will work. For instance, if you are a practitioner of ceremonial magic, you might choose to do a Lesser Banishing Ritual or circumambulation with the elements in each room. If your are a root worker or a folk magic practitioner, a bath made with sage, chamomile lavender and a small amount of vinegar can be used on the floor, door and windows. Most important is that you focus your mind and body on the act of purifying the space. Eventually, the frequency of cleansings will depend on how much work you have done, who is coming into your space and—most importantly listen to your gut.

When wood is magical

What is the best tree to harvest wood from for making a wand?—Submitted by Arlana Hensley

The making of wands is very specific in some magical traditions and not so much in others. If you are new on your path and are working with a Coven or Magical Lodge the first suggestion is the obvious one—check in with officiating leader or elders of the group. Once you have been given some direction, ask them the whys and the wherefores. Don't be shy. If your path is a solitary one there are a number of choices for you to decide on.

Many traditions of Ceremonial Magic require that the wand be made from the wood of a fruit bearing tree, with a heavy leaning towards almond, more than likely because Aaron in Exodus was said to have made his rod from the almond tree. The tradition is to identify the tree that

190

you will use, pruning a suitable branch. The branch is then hewn with a single blow. There are many ways in which to process and purify the newly made wand.

If you are of the Pagan or Wiccan persuasion, many will use apple, rowan or willow to make their wands. Each of these trees have an strong association with Goddess traditions. That being said, not all operate by these rules. In some traditions there is a wand tradition in which the wand is tipped with a pinecone in a very deliberate fashion to make it male. If this is the case, pine, oak or alder might work better.

In all cases, if you are choosing to use a branch from a living tree, try to be respectful and gracious at the very least. Many traditions require that you leave an offering as payment.

It's all symbolic

I have seen many photographs of Witches and other magical practitioners standing in a double circle with symbols drawn in between the two circles. Is this something I should be doing?—Submitted by Jennifer Miller

The flavor of your practices more than likely will indicate how to set-up your ritual space. The use of a circle as sacred space is common to most traditions of Wicca. As for Pagan practices, some use a magical circle some do not. If the Pagan practice has its roots in Wicca more than likely they subscribe to the use of a Circle for sacred space. Practices such as Heathen, Hellenic, Roman or Fairy for the most part do not use Circles.

To the use of a double Circle, considering the above you have a choice to make. In many Wiccan traditions, a single Circle is used. However there are traditions that might use the double Circle—there are some Alexandrians that do use the double circle. Ceremonial magicians do sometimes use double circles. Those that are lodge based organizations tend not to. Your choice should be based on some of the above and you should inform yourself further through reading and consulting with others on your same path.

Let us hear from you, too

We love to hear from our readers. Letters should be sent with the writer's name (or just first name or initials), address, daytime phone number and e-mail address, if available. Published material may be edited for clarity or length. All letters and e-mails will become the property of The Witches' Almanac Ltd. *and will not be returned. We regret that due to the volume of correspondence we cannot reply to all communications.*

The Witches' Almanac, Ltd.
P.O. Box 25239
Providence, RI 02905-7700
info@TheWitchesAlmanac.com
www.TheWitchesAlmanac.com

Discover a Mythical Mystical Realm of
Books, Incense, Candles, Crystals, Oils, Tarot,
Gemstone & Symbolic Jewelry, Statuary, Talismans,
Oracles, Pendulums, Runes, Clothing
& All Things Rare & Magickal...

All Things Rare & Magickal

Classes - Events - Psychic Readings
Spiritual Consultaions & Candle Dressing

AVALONBEYOND.COM
1211 Hillcrest St. Orlando Florida 32803 407 895 7439
-Over 20 Years of Magickal Service -

The products and services offered above are paid advertisements.

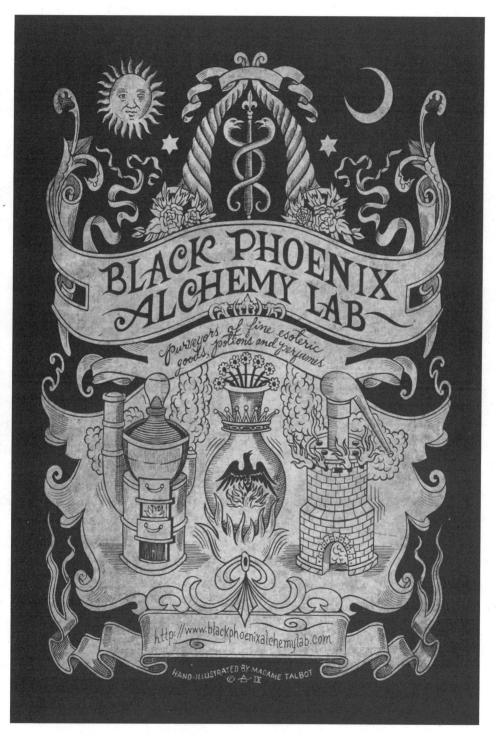

BLACK PHOENIX ALCHEMY LAB

purveyors of fine esoteric goods, potions and perfumes

http://www.blackphoenixalchemylab.com

HAND-ILLUSTRATED BY MADAME TALBOT

The products and services offered above are paid advertisements.

836   836

The
Coven
Of All Altars

www.allaltars.org

Honoring the Life and Legacy of a Wiccan Trailblazer

You've read his books. Now learn about the man. Christine Cunningham Ashworth, Scott Cunningham's sister, offers tales and memories from her life with Scott. Featuring Cunningham family photos, the book also contains contributions from some of witchcraft's leading lights, including Mat Auryn, Amy Blackthorn, Dorothy Morrison, and more.

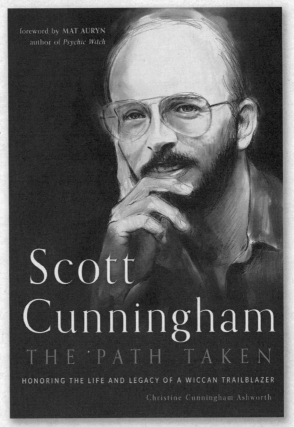

September 2023 • ISBN: 9781578638086 • $21.95 • 6 x 9 • 240 pages • Paperback

WEISER BOOKS

800.423.7087   orders@rwwbooks.com

The products and services offered above are paid advertisements.

❧MARKETPLACE ❧

www.AzureGreen.net Jewelry, Amulets, Incense, Oils, Herbs, Candles, Statuary, Gemstones, Ritual Items. Wholesale inquiries welcome.

Voodoo Queen specializing in removal and reversal of evil spells. Be careful of what you wish for before you call me: **678-677-1144**

Wendy Wildcraft Herbal Apothecary. Wild gifts and botanical wisdom to inspire the body, mind and spirit. **(978) 219-9453**, info@wendywildcraft.com, www.wendywildcraft.com

The Crystal Fox 311 Main Street, Laurel, MD 20707 USA. The largest new age/metaphysical gift shop in the mid-Atlantic region. Monday-Saturday 10am-9pm Sunday 11am-7pm. **(301) 317-1980**, cryfox@verizon.net, www.TheCrystalFox.biz

The products and services offered above are paid advertisements.

TO: The Witches' Almanac
P.O. Box 1292, Newport, RI 02840-9998
www.TheWitchesAlmanac.com

Email (required) _____

Name_____

Address_____

City_____ State_____ Zip_____

WITCHCRAFT being by nature one of the secretive arts, it may not be as easy to find us next year. If you'd like to make sure we know where you are, why don't you send us your name, email address and street address? You will certainly hear from us.

Dikki-Jo Mullen

The Witches' Almanac Astrologer
skymaiden@juno.com
Sky Maiden Musings dikkijomullen.wordpress.com
Star Dates Astrology Forecasts facebook.com/dikkijo.mullen
Dikki Jo Mullen on **YouTube**

**Seminars, Presentations,
Convention Programs**

Complete Astrology & Parapsychology Services

Paranormal Investigations

*(see the website for astrology articles
and information about upcoming events)*

The products and services offered above are paid advertisements.

The Witches' Almanac 2024
Wall Calendar

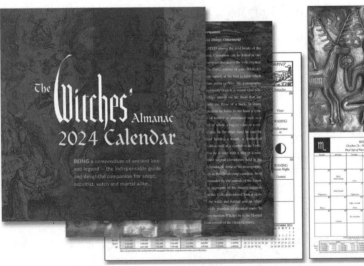

The ever popular Moon Calendar in each issue of The Witches' Almanac is a wall calendar as well. Providing the standard Moon phases, channeled actions and an expanded version of the topic featured in the Moon Calendar are now available in a full-size wall calendar.

Aradia
Gospel of the Witches
Charles Godfrey Leland

ARADIA IS THE FIRST work in English in which witch-craft is portrayed as an underground old religion, surviving in secret from ancient Pagan times.

- Used as a core text by many modern Neo-Pagans.
- Foundation material containing traditional witchcraft practices
- This special edition features appreciations by such authors as Paul Huson, Raven Grimassi, Judika Illes, Michael Howard, Christopher Penczak, Myth Woodling, Christina Oakley Harrington, Patricia Della-Piana, Jimahl di Fiosa and Donald Weiser. A beautiful and compelling work, this edition is an up to date format, while keeping the text unchanged. 172 pages $16.95

The ABC of Magic Charms
Elizabeth Pepper

Mankind has sought protection from mysterious forces beyond mortal control. Humans have sought the help of animal, mineral, vegetable. The enlarged edition of *Magic Charms from A to Z*, guides us in calling on these forces. $12.95

The Little Book of Magical Creatures
Elizabeth Pepper and Barbara Stacy

AN UPDATE of the classic *Magical Creatures*, featuring Animals Tame, Animals Wild, Animals Fabulous—plus an added section of enchanting animal myths from other times, other places. *A must for all animal lovers.* $12.95

The Witchcraft of Dame Darrel of York
Charles Godfrey Leland, Introduction by Robert Mathiesen

A beautifully reproduced facsimile of the illuminated manuscript shedding light on the basis for a modern practice. A treasured by those practicing Pagans, as well as scholars.   Standard Hardcover $65.00 or Exclusive full leather bound, numbered and slipcased edition $145.00

DAME FORTUNE'S WHEEL TAROT: A PICTORIAL KEY
Paul Huson

 Based upon Paul Huson's research in *Mystical Origins of the Tarot, Dame Fortune's Wheel Tarot* illustrates for the first time the earliest, traditional Tarot card interpretations as collected in the 1700s by Jean-Baptiste Alliette. In addition to detailed descriptions, full color reproductions of Huson's original designs for all 79 cards.

WITCHES ALL

A Treasury from past editions, is a collection from *The Witches' Almanac* publications of the past. Arranged by topics, the book, like the popular almanacs, is thought provoking and often spurs the reader on to a tangent leading to even greater discovery. It's perfect for study or casual reading,

GREEK GODS IN LOVE

 Barbara Stacy casts a marvelously original eye on the beloved stories of Greek deities, replete with amorous oddities and escapades. We relish these tales in all their splendor and antic humor, and offer an inspired storyteller's fresh version of the old, old mythical magic.

MAGIC CHARMS FROM A TO Z

A treasury of amulets, talismans, fetishes and other lucky objects compiled by the staff of *The Witches' Almanac*. An invaluable guide for all who respond to the call of mystery and enchantment.

LOVE CHARMS

 Love has many forms, many aspects. Ceremonies performed in witchcraft celebrate the joy and the blessings of love. Here is a collection of love charms to use now and ever after.

MAGICAL CREATURES

Mystic tradition grants pride of place to many members of the animal kingdom. Some share our life. Others live wild and free. Still others never lived at all, springing instead from the remarkable power of human imagination.

ANCIENT ROMAN HOLIDAYS

The glory that was Rome awaits you in Barbara Stacy's classic presentation of a festive year in Pagan times. Here are the gods and goddesses as the Romans conceived them, accompanied by the annual rites performed in their worship. Scholarly, lighthearted – a rare combination.

CELTIC TREE MAGIC

Robert Graves in *The White Goddess* writes of the significance of trees in the old Celtic lore. *Celtic Tree Magic* is an investigation of the sacred trees in the remarkable Beth-Luis-Nion alphabet and their role in folklore, poetry and mysticism.

MOON LORE

As both the largest and the brightest object in the night sky, and the only one to appear in phases, the Moon has been a rich source of myth for as long as there have been mythmakers.

MAGIC SPELLS
AND INCANTATIONS

Words have magic power. Their sound, spoken or sung, has ever been a part of mystic ritual. From ancient Egypt to the present, those who practice the art of enchantment have drawn inspiration from a treasury of thoughts and themes passed down through the ages.

LOVE FEASTS

Creating meals to share with the one you love can be a sacred ceremony in itself. With the Witch in mind, culinary adept Christine Fox offers magical menus and recipes for every month in the year.

RANDOM RECOLLECTIONS
III, IV

Pages culled from the original (no longer available) issues of *The Witches' Almanac,* published annually throughout the 1970s, are now available in a series of tasteful booklets. A treasure for those who missed us the first time around, keepsakes for those who remember.

Liber Spirituum

BEING A TRUE AND FAITHFUL REPRODUCTION OF
The Grimoire of Paul Huson

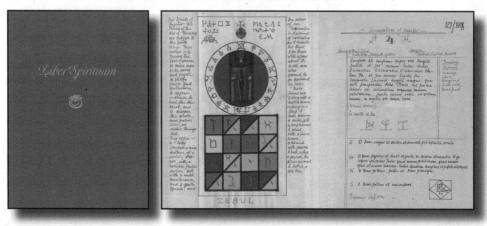

In 1966, as an apprentice mage, Paul Huson began the work of constructing his personal *Liber Spirituum* or *Book of Spirits*. The origins of his work in fact have their genesis a number of years before he took up the pen to illuminate the pages of his *Book of Spirits*. It was in his tender youth that Paul's interest in matters magical began. It was his insatiable curiosity and thirst for knowledge that would eventually lead him to knock on the doors of Dion Fortune's Society of the Inner Light in 1964, as well as studying the practices of the Hermetic Order of the Golden Dawn and the Stella Matutina under the aegis of Israel Regardie. Drawing on this wellspring of knowledge and such venerable works as the *Key of Solomon, The Magus, Heptameron, Three Books of Occult Philosophy* as well as others set down a unique and informed set of rituals, in addition to employing his own artistry in the creation of distinctive imagery.

Using the highest quality photographic reproduction and printing methods, Paul's personal grimoire has here been faithfully and accurately reproduced for the first time. In addition to preserving the ink quality and use of gold and silver paint, this facsimile reproduction has maintained all of Huson's corrections, including torn, pasted, missing pages and his hand drawn and renumbered folios. Preserved as well are the unique characteristics of the original grimoire paper as it has aged through the decades. In this way, the publisher has stayed true to Paul Huson's *Book of Spirits* as it was originally drawn and painted.

223 Pages
Paperback — $59.95
Hardbound in slipcase — $149.95

For further imformation visit: TheWitchesAlmanac.com

204

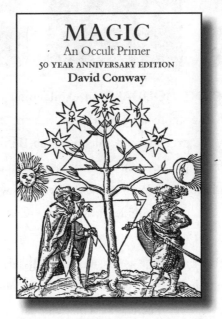

Ancient Holidays Series

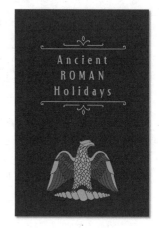

INTRODUCING ANCIENT HOLIDAYS, an exhilarating new book series that immerses readers into the captivating world of ancient civilizations' spiritual calendars. Authored by the exceptionally talented Mab Borden, these books offer profound and enlightening journeys through the sacred calendars of the ancient Egyptians, Greeks, and Romans. With great excitement, we present this series, confident that it will not only provide invaluable knowledge but also kindle inspiration for our own spiritual observations.

Within each captivating title of the series, readers will delve into comprehensive explanations of the months and seasons, gaining profound insights into the significance of sacred days. Every sacred day is meticulously detailed, encompassing the deity being honored and the social and ritual activities associated with it. Additionally, each publication is enriched with information-packed appendices, which provide a wealth of knowledge, including the mapping of deity holidays to the corresponding seasons.

For futher details and to order visit us at:
TheWitchesAlmanac.com/pages/the-ancient-holiday-series

ORDER FORM

Each timeless edition of *The Witches' Almanac* is unique.
Limited numbers of previous years' editions are available.

Item	Price	Qty.	Total
2024-2025 The Witches' Almanac – Fire: Forging Freedom	$13.95		
2023-2024 The Witches' Almanac – Earth: Origin of Chthonic Powers	$13.95		
2022-2023 The Witches' Almanac – The Moon: Transforming the Inner Spirit	$12.95		
2021-2022 The Witches' Almanac – The Sun: Rays of Hope	$12.95		
2020-2021 The Witches' Almanac – Stones: The Foundation of Earth	$12.95		
2019-2020 The Witches' Almanac – Animals: Friends & Familiars	$12.95		
2018-2019 The Witches' Almanac – The Magic of Plants	$12.95		
2017-2018 The Witches' Almanac – Water: Our Primal Source	$12.95		
2016-2017 The Witches' Almanac – Air: the Breath of Life	$12.95		
2014-2015 The Witches' Almanac – Mystic Earth	$12.95		
2013-2014 The Witches' Almanac – Wisdom of the Moon	$11.95		
2012-2013 The Witches' Almanac – Radiance of the Sun	$11.95		
2011-2012 The Witches' Almanac – Stones, Powers of Earth	$11.95		
2010-2011 The Witches' Almanac – Animals Great & Small	$11.95		
2009-2010 The Witches' Almanac – Plants & Healing Herbs	$11.95		
2008-2009 The Witches' Almanac – Divination & Prophecy	$10.95		
2007-2008 The Witches' Almanac – The Element of Water	$9.95		
1993-2006 issues of The Witches' Almanac	$10.00		
The Witches' Almanac 50 Year Anniversary Edition, paperback	$15.95		
The Witches' Almanac 50 Year Anniversary Edition, hardbound	$24.95		
2023-2024 The Witches' Almanac Wall Calendar	$14.95		
SALE: Bundle I—8 Almanac back issues (1991, 1993–1999)	$50.00		
Bundle II—10 Almanac back issues (2000–2009)	$65.00		
Bundle III—10 Almanac back issues (2010–2019)	$100.00		
Bundle IV—30 Almanac back issues (1993–2022)	$199.00		
Ancient Egyptian Holidays	$16.95		
Ancient Greek Holidays	$18.95		
Ancient Roman Holidays	$19.95		
Liber Spirituum—The Grimoire of Paul Huson, paperback	$59.95		
Liber Spirituum—The Grimoire of Paul Huson, hardbound in slipcase	$149.95		
Dame Fortune's Wheel Tarot: A Pictorial Key	$19.95		
Magic: An Occult Primer—50 Year Anniversary Edition, paperback	$24.95		
Magic: An Occult Primer—50 Year Anniversary Edition, hardbound	$29.95		
The Witches' Almanac Coloring Book	$12.00		
The Witchcraft of Dame Darrel of York, clothbound, signed and numbered, in slip case	$85.00		
The Witchcraft of Dame Darrel of York, leatherbound, signed and numbered, in slip case	$145.00		
Aradia or The Gospel of the Witches	$16.95		
The Horned Shepherd	$16.95		
The ABC of Magic Charms	$12.95		

Item	Price	Qty.	Total
The Little Book of Magical Creatures	$12.95		
Greek Gods in Love	$15.95		
Witches All	$13.95		
Ancient Roman Holidays (original first printing)	$9.95		
Celtic Tree Magic	$9.95		
Love Charms	$9.95		
Love Feasts	$9.95		
Magic Charms from A to Z	$12.95		
Magical Creatures	$12.95		
Magic Spells and Incantations	$12.95		
Moon Lore	$9.95		
Random Recollections Volumes III and IV	$9.95		
The Rede of the Wiccae – Hardcover	$49.95		
The Rede of the Wiccae – Softcover	$22.95		
Keepers of the Flame	$20.95		
Sounds of Infinity	$24.95		
The Magic of Herbs	$24.95		
Harry M. Hyatt's Works on Hoodoo and Folklore: A Full Reprint in 13 Volumes (including audio download) *Hoodoo—Conjuration—Witchcraft—Rootwork*	$1,400.00		
Single volumes are also available starting at	$120.0		
Subtotal			
Tax *(7% sales tax for RI customers)*			
Shipping & Handling *(See shipping rates section)*			
TOTAL			

MISCELLANY			
Item	Price	QTY.	Total
Sterling Silver Colophon	$35.00		
Pouch	$3.95		
Skull Scarf	$20.00		
Hooded Sweatshirt, Blk	$30.00		
Hooded Sweatshirt, Red	$30.00		
L-Sleeve T, Black	$15.00		
L-Sleeve T, Red	$15.00		
S-Sleeve T, Black/W	$15.00		
S-Sleeve T, Black/R	$15.00		

MISCELLANY			
Item	Price	QTY.	Total
S-Sleeve T, Dk H/R	$15.00		
S-Sleeve T, Dk H/W	$15.00		
S-Sleeve T, Red/B	$15.00		
S-Sleeve T, Ash/R	$15.00		
S-Sleeve T, Purple/W	$15.00		
Magnets – set of 3	$1.50		
Subtotal			
Tax (7% for RI Customers)			
Shipping and Handling (call for estimate)			
Total			

Payment available by check or money order payable in U.S. funds or credit card or PayPal

The Witches' Almanac, Ltd., PO Box 25239, Providence, RI 02905-7700

(401) 847-3388 (phone) • (888) 897-3388 (fax)
Email: info@TheWitchesAlmanac.com • www.TheWitchesAlmanac.com